Douglas Board has enjoyed a backsta̶ ̶ ̶into Britain's power bases for 30 years. For more than two decades a gatekeeper for some of the country's high places, in 2010 he received a doctorate in how we choose leaders. He has been a leader himself and is currently a coach for a number of senior executives.

Douglas received a first-class honours degree in mathematics from Cambridge University, followed by a scholarship to Harvard for his master's. After working in Whitehall he joined Saxton Bampfylde, a leading UK executive search firm, of which he became deputy chairman. He was a trustee, and then treasurer, of the Diana, Princess of Wales Memorial Fund, and for six years chaired Britain's largest refugee charity, the Refugee Council. Currently he is one of the five non-legal members of the Queen's Counsel Selection Panel; the Church of England's external adviser in renewing its selection process for priests-in-training; and an honorary senior visiting fellow at the business school of City, University of London.

He lives in London and, when possible, in Johannesburg. He usually says that he has published four books (all on leadership – two applied research books and two satirical novels) but in truth his first published book, in Hong Kong at the age of nineteen, was a maths textbook. He likes to explain things.

This book couldn't be more timely. It explains how the barely competent but entitled occupy elite positions in our organisations and in society in general. It illuminates the endless round of board appointments after evident failure. It's also practical, full of tips for navigating the devious complexities of corporate hierarchies.
Gareth Jones, author of Why Should Anyone Be Led by You? *and visiting professor, IE Madrid*

Elites gives a no-bullshit new lens through which to view the workplace. Surely 'wizards' and 'muggle crust' must now enter the management lexicon?
Lynne Embleton, CEO, IAG Cargo

It would be a mistake to put a 'business book' label on *Elites*. After a year of pandemic-triggered lockdowns and sacrifices by many, this comes at just the right time to challenge how we think about the world and ourselves. I found myself rechecking my answers to some of the bigger questions the book invites us to ponder – about purpose, what success means, who we are and what is important to each of us.
Fields Wicker-Miurin OBE, board director and social entrepreneur

I can't stand most leadership books but I love *Elites*. It offers a unique lens which will change the way you view the whole vista of work, and what separates those at the very top from the rest of us.
Jonathan Morgan, headhunter

The book forced me to think about who and what the 'elites' are; and where and how in my working life I have fitted (or not) into this classification. Overall, a deeply searching and satisfying work.
Mark Lewis, international lawyer

Brilliant: the ultimate travel guide to power in the world of work; packed with places to see, things to do and lots of shared personal experience. At the end you feel that you know this new terrain and are eager to explore it further, no longer fearful of the unknown or trapped by previously held perceptions.
Niall Trafford, former CEO, BRE Group

A witty and irreverent insider's reflection on the mysteries of climbing to 'the top'. This guide shines light on what is prized and what is shunned – often the same thing – during trials of ascension.
Hugh Willmott FBA, research professor of organisation studies, Cardiff University

I wish I could have read it in 2003 when I started work as associate dean at the business school. I got irritated by people who were nothing like as good as they thought they were, but after reading this book I now understand them so much better.
David Sims, emeritus professor of organisational behaviour, the business school (formerly Cass) at City, University of London

A fascinating read: part insider guide, part critique, part reflection on what really matters. An insightful book which should be read by anyone who wants to think about purpose in our increasingly competitive world of work and their place in it.
Chris Mowles, professor of complexity and management, University of Hertfordshire

An accessible and compelling account of the faith and witness which enabled the author to journey through an environment in which many fear to tread. Douglas appeals to the inherent capacity that each one of us has to use our God-given talents, common sense and hard work to help us climb the hills and mountains of power.
Most Revd Dr Thabo Makgoba, Archbishop of Cape Town

Of the many valuable things Douglas Board does in this brilliant, unusual book, two stand out. He helps us see through our elites – never to denigrate but nonetheless to reveal that they are just another tribe, no less and no more valuable than all others. And in doing this, he exposes a deeper truth. He elegantly skewers our individualistic and atomised vision of ourselves, offering instead a far richer, more vivid and more human vision of what leadership and its greatest triumphs can be.
Nick Wilkie, third sector leader

ELITES

*Can you rise to the top
without losing your soul?*

Douglas Board

EYE BOOKS
NON-FICTION

Published by Eye Books
29A Barrow Street
Much Wenlock
Shropshire
TF13 6EN

www.eye-books.com

First edition 2021
Copyright © Douglas Board 2021

Cover design by Nell Wood
Graphic icons courtesy of vecteezy.com
Typeset in Bembo Std.

All rights reserved. Apart from brief extracts for the purpose of review, no part of this publication may be reproduced, stored in a retrieval system, or transmitted in any form or by any means, electronic, mechanical, photocopying, recording or otherwise without permission of the publisher.

Douglas Board has asserted his right under the Copyright, Designs and Patents Act 1988 to be identified as author of this work.

British Library Cataloguing in Publication Data
A catalogue record for this book is available from the British Library

Printed by CPI Group (UK) Ltd, Croydon CR0 4YY

ISBN 9781785632228

Contents

PART ONE:
A GUIDE TO THE SURVIVAL GUIDE
(Essential preparation)

Glossary	13
Introduction	17
The room where it happens	19
How this book works	23

PART TWO:
THE SENIOR EXECUTIVE'S SURVIVAL GUIDE
(Lessons for climbing to the top)

Three lessons about reality	37
1 More beats less	39
2 The rational isn't personal	49
3 Reality is simple	57

Three lessons about relationships   63
   4 Be transparent   65
   5 Defer to bosses and clients   73
   6 Take responsibility   79

Four lessons about advancement   83
   7 Learn stuff   87
   8 Get feedback   99
   9 Don't fail   103
   10 The route to the top is open   109

Three action takeaways   115
   11 How to survive elites   117
   12 How to join elites   123
   13 How to change elites (1)   135

PART THREE:
BIG QUESTIONS
(What really makes us want to reach the top)

And breathe…   143
Exploring society   145
Who am I?   151
The eleventh lesson   157
What success turns out to mean for me   165
The magic show of elites   173
The fourth action takeaway: How to change elites (2)   179
Rising and thriving without losing your soul   187

END NOTES:
REVIEWING THE CLIMB
(Back at base camp)

Our journey revisited   195

Suggested books   201

Acknowledgements   205

PART ONE

A GUIDE
TO THE
SURVIVAL GUIDE

(Essential preparation)

PART ONE

A Guide
to the
Survival Mode

(General preparation)

Glossary

Meritocracy
An organisation, professional field or wider group activity in which the opportunity to advance is open to all and based on hard work, learning and results. 'Advance' means rising in peer respect, being offered prestigious opportunities or being appointed to senior positions.

Elites/wizards
The top tier of individuals within a meritocracy: the elite is the group, its members are wizards. In an organisation, this is its pre-eminent executives; in a freelance activity it is the players most admired by their peers; in a sales activity it's 'rainmakers' – magnets who attract enough business to pay for many salaries.

Glass ceiling

The boundary between wizards and the tier below them. The boundary is hard to see. On crossing it, the 'rules of the game' change in an undeclared way.

Muggle crust

The tier below wizards in a meritocracy; the senior executives who most often bump into the glass ceiling. This tier hides some of the best leaders, managers and professionals, but the muggle crust mindset encourages the belief that they belong where they are, and that wizardry is not for them. They are this book's hidden heroes.

Muggles

The large group of grafters in a meritocracy who have climbed a few rungs of the ladder but not got to the top. The lowest muggles are quite junior, but not the bottom of the heap. Through hard work, loyalty, commitment and luck, they might advance.

Muggle badges

Things which, without the wearer's knowledge, identify him/her as a muggle to wizards, ie, 'not one of us'. Part of how the glass ceiling works.

Artisans

Players whose engagement in an activity carries no special authority or prestige; frontline workers, the largest group in a meritocracy.

Princelings
Players in a meritocracy at least one of whose parents is a wizard. Even if princelings start at entry level, they may benefit from their parent's connections.

Pixie dust
One of the things the muggle crust needs to become wizards; introductions by wizards to other wizards and help in establishing their profile.

Power
Usually understood as what enables you to get more of what you want. Typically, 'what you want' is left unexamined, which can be dangerous to your soul.

Soul
What to you is most special about being human.

Introduction

THIS BOOK IS ABOUT MAGIC. Magic is about illusion, and standing in the wings is a small group of people who are admitted into the secret. In this book Douglas Board is going to admit *you* into the secret of the magic of elites: the trick by which we give too much respect to a small group of people who believe they deserve it.

Exposing a magic trick can be done in a few different ways; Douglas wants to do it in a fun way. You are more likely to enjoy the ride, and stick with him to the end, even though in a few places your brain might hurt (because the ideas are difficult, not because they have been poorly explained).

So, welcome inside our theatre. While you wait for the show to start, you see a few curious objects on stage (the glossary). Then an MC comes on and makes an introduction. The MC can't be a famous person because famous people might be tricksy wizards. What's needed is someone who can't bear bullshit – that's me. So maybe the show isn't bullshit either.

Let me introduce Douglas. I went to him for coaching after hitting a wall at work. He helped me see that I could play the game differently, and that if I chose to I could not only rise, but thrive. He will start with a true story about something as rare as a white hippo (the righteous departure of the CEO of a top-fifty company). As he tells that story you will sense who he is, why he is on stage and above all, his motivation for what he is writing, which is in part memoir. Something about empowerment, justice for hidden heroes, and happier individuals in a better society. But at this stage these are suggestions we glimpse, rather than grasp fully.

Then the show proper begins. Part Two is a series of lessons which reveal meritocratic elites – who they are, what they are and how to survive them – by unpacking their magic tricks. Then comes Part Three, in which Douglas tells us that the exposé in Part Two unleashes a Pandora's Box of big questions, questions which go to the heart of what it is to be an ordinary human being, hungry for respect and happiness. Because the secret of elites is that they are surprisingly ordinary. And what that means for me and you – wherever we see ourselves and wherever anyone else sees us on the spectrum of ordinary to elite – is that the answers may strike close to home.

Go on, get the popcorn. Enjoy the show.

Jo Hill
Director, financial regulation

The room where
it happens

THE SOUND OF HUBRIS shattering can be very satisfying, even if you are not in the room where it happens. Henry was the CEO of one of Britain's top fifty employers. When top bosses get axed, they usually reappear in another boardroom near you, but this time was different. It began like this:

Henry's No. 2 and chief of operations quit for greener pastures, leaving a gaping hole which would take recruiters months to fill. Henry needed an existing member of his senior team to hold the fort – to carry on doing their own job and run operations as well. He picked Katharine, his finance director and one of the people I was coaching.

What followed for Katharine was a year of 5-9 days (that's 5am to 9pm) and weekends with no time for her kid. But she was a corporate hero. As a No. 2, cheer-leading and making her boss look good came naturally. At the same time, she led her organisation's daily fight for survival and profit. Success and failure were measured in decimal points of margin and market share. For working both jobs, her reward was a temporary ten per cent salary hike.

Come the end of the year, she inducted the new hire – a man who had spent most of the previous twelve months on 'gardening leave'. When he arrived at Henry's company, he was paid more than Katharine's hiked salary. It was said of Fred Astaire and Ginger Rogers that Ginger did everything Fred did, but backwards and in high heels. To which we can add 'and got paid less'.

But look, Henry did say thank you. He told Katharine to expect a special bonus. The company was no bank so the bonus wouldn't be Lamborghini-sized, but it was the thought that counted. When the time came but nothing arrived in her bank account, Katharine asked the relevant salary administrator (many grades her junior) if the money had been delayed. 'No,' was the puzzled reply. 'You can't be getting a special bonus, because Henry hasn't given you a top performance marking.' The company's rule was crystal clear: employees had to be classed as top performers in order to get any special bonus.

Katharine was shocked; so was I when she told me. Pretending for a few weeks to pay a bonus and then not delivering was as pointless as it was mean. When confronted, Henry pushed the blame upstairs, to the remuneration committee of the board of directors. This was equally pointless: in little more than a day Katharine established that the committee had not changed Henry's recommendation. Some weeks later Henry departed to spend time with his family. In reality, he had been told to go. Many factors were involved – the performance of the business as a whole was far from stellar – but Henry had misjudged things badly. The directors knew Katharine better and trusted her more than Henry had realised.

When justice got done – when the directors spoke to Henry and when the dishonesty stopped – I wasn't in the room. Metaphorically speaking I was holding Katharine's towel in the corridor outside. The sound of shattering hubris was no less gratifying for that; in corporate life you don't hear it often. While my coachee fought her own fights, the time we spent together helped her first to see, and then have confidence, that the world at the top works a bit differently than she thought; that she had more power than she realised. I was also able to help her think through her options and consider what kind of person she wished to be.

If you are a senior executive like Katharine, being loyal and taking responsibility can put you at risk. You need a *survival guide*. So Part Two of this book lays out my best shot at how the top levels of organisations work, demonstrating how you can survive and thrive as a senior executive with your principles intact.

However, lifting the lid on corporate summitry brings to the front a hornet's nest of *big questions*. If the pattern described in Part Two is true, what drives it? How wide does the pattern spread? Why bother aspiring to the top? Could we organise the world differently? In Part Three, I chase down these questions, which have everything to do with the ordinary humanity all of us share.

Regardless of your ambition or position, Part Three could prompt a change in how you perceive your own life. Writing it certainly did that for me. Let's think again about how the words 'room' and 'corridor' appear in my telling of Henry and Katharine's story.

Who hasn't, as the musical *Hamilton* puts it, wanted to be in 'the room where it happens' – in a place of influence and proximity to important decisions? Being a recruiter gave me that chance when critical hiring decisions were made. Eventually I stepped outside the meeting rooms of the powerful to see other places and do other things. I did not know where I would end up, and made the change with mixed feelings. I put those feelings into a soundtrack for my leaving party: the surging energy of the Waterboys' 'That Was The River, This Is The Sea' embraced the future while Billy Joel's 'Say Goodbye To Hollywood' lingered wistfully on the past.

Writing Part Three of this book turned my understanding upside down. What happens in the rooms of the powerful will always deserve respect, because they can do the rest of us much good or ill. A wider range of people should be able to get into those rooms and make decisive contributions. But while the rooms of power may be splendid, who says that the rest of us are living in corridors? I did; I told myself that; I said it because it was obvious.

It was also wrong. If the point of Part Two is to put unsparingly in view the ordinariness of extraordinary people, Part Three tries to put equally in view the extraordinariness of 'ordinary' people. Unleashing the extraordinariness of 'ordinary' human beings happens one person at a time. Being a coach lets me be the lucky one in the room when *that* happens with my coachees. Perhaps this book will let me be in the room where it happens with you.

How this book works

EACH SECTION OF THIS BOOK is marked with one of three symbols. The first represents a **detective story of ideas**. Magic works by leading us to take as obvious something which isn't true. To unscramble our thinking, we will follow closely a small number of key ideas. We're also going to shift our gaze a fraction away from where we usually look. In order to understand elites, we're going to look really closely at individuals who are nearly at the top, but not quite.

By elites I mean groups of individuals (I'm calling them wizards) right at the top of their field of activity, be that managing an organisation, running a country or performing music or sport. Especially in Part Two we will concentrate on those kinds of organisations and activities in which – apparently – anyone can become a wizard if they work hard, learn stuff and achieve results. These activities are meritocracies.

Some wizards are famous, for example Jeff Bezos, Margaret Atwood and Kendrick Lamar; however, people who are famous are not necessarily wizards. (Prince Andrew, for example.) But most wizards are much closer to your workplace and your life than this. We'll shortly see how to spot one.

As well as wizards, you will hear me talk a lot about 'muggles' and the 'muggle crust'. I need to say something about this language. Talking magic is an obvious reason to borrow a word like 'muggle'. A fine English word which, in 1600, meant 'sweetheart', was given by JK Rowling a really useful new meaning – human beings without magic powers. (I should make clear that neither Rowling nor anyone connected with the Harry Potter franchise has endorsed *Elites*.) Rowling's meaning is useful because it carries the sting of disregard, like lemon juice on a cut. Already we understand something about how wizards think of muggles, before we've even begun.

I chose 'muggle crust' to describe the topmost muggle layer because they're trapped under a glass ceiling and at risk of becoming burned out or congealed – think of a crème brûlée. I am much more muggle crust than wizard, so if the terms disturb you, let me explain what I'm about. We're following the example of other groups who created proud identities out of 'black' and 'queer'. Words matter. If one group tells another, 'I hear your sneer but it doesn't frighten me', then the balance of power between them shifts.

Which brings us to power. Henry's story on page 19 is easy to re-tell in power language (as in, he had a lot of power but not as much as he thought). But once more, we will take a different way into our subject, and make little use of this word until the end. Again, our chief obstacle in the detective story of ideas will prove to be obvious ways of thinking which turn out to be incorrect. The obvious way to think about power turns life into a card game. We peer over the characters' shoulders (Henry's, or Katharine's) to see the cards which they have been dealt, and toy with different ways of playing their hands. Instead, our gaze in Part Two of this book will be closely directed towards what's obvious to Henry and what's obvious to my coachee. We'll still be thinking about power, but differently. At the end of the book we will see why the obvious way to think about power is dangerous to our souls.

Sections of this book which describe life at or near organisational or professional peaks or which offer practical advice begin with the summit symbol.

If our focus is going to be on individuals within arm's reach of the top but not quite there – the muggle crust – what do those jobs look like? In different work places they carry different titles but common ones include 'head of ...' or 'director of ...'. Enviable amounts of money may be paid.

Often the people in these roles pinch themselves, having shot up much higher than they had imagined they would when they were twenty. But normally you won't find these individuals' names and photographs in their organisations' annual reports. They are too busy backstage working out how to deliver the promises made by the names and shiny faces which do appear. It can be heroic work. It's also unsung and dangerous.

For example, imagine being in charge of a line on the London Underground. I've never met these individuals, but Transport for London publishes a directory of every job in the organisation which pays more than £50,000 a year. The 2018 edition runs to 881 pages; the higher the page number, the higher the salary. On page 868 we get to:

Head of Line Operations A key member of the Line Operations directorate leadership team, accountable for delivering a reliable, safe and customer-focused line operation on one or more LU lines, whilst ensuring high levels of engagement with customers, staff and trade unions. Responsible for continuously improving performance in the areas of customer service, safety, reliability and financial efficiency, contributing to the delivery of a world class network operation. Showing personal and inspirational functional leadership, advocating modernisation and transformation to create a 'can do' culture across your line(s). Working collaboratively with Customer Operations, Asset Operations and Network Delivery to deliver a world class customer experience. Accountable for ensuring that the employee relations landscape is constructively managed and business change is effectively implemented. Salary £120,000 – £124,999.

This job is 868 rungs up an 881-rung ladder, but it's not quite at the top. We're not told the job-holder's name. Just six pages later that changes. The salaries reach £150,000 and each job-holder's name appears. *Now* we've reached the top.

Part Two of *Elites* provides ten lessons and three takeaways which describe how to climb to – and survive on – page 868 of corporate life; and how to aim, if you want to, towards page 881. In other words, starting with junior muggles and ending with wizards. Each lesson is fundamental to advancing your career in a meritocratic environment – which means a (mostly) fair workplace in which advancement is based on results, ability and effort. The lessons look obvious: working hard, pleasing bosses and clients, taking responsibility, learning more. But they're deceptive.

The 'obvious' truth of each lesson changes as we rise to the top. First, we'll see that to rise up we have no choice but to learn the lesson deeply, so that it becomes ingrained. Then we'll notice how the lesson deceives. Once ingrained, it marks you out to your bosses as 'not one of them'. It might tell gatekeepers (like headhunters) that you are 'not ready' to join the elite. It may even tell you what muggle crust often tell themselves – 'I was ready to be put in my place, and that place wasn't at the top'.

To be clear, 'the top' doesn't have to be marked out by suit-wearing or corner offices (although Buckingham Palace was awash in pin-stripes when I went there to pitch an executive search to two sirs and a lord). The *de rigueur* for your elites may be hipster beards and no job titles, or a general's stars worn on the collar – that's irrelevant. What matters is having to bust your gut working hard, pleasing bosses and clients, taking responsibility and learning stuff to stand a chance of becoming one.

Elites is also a short **memoir**. I wasn't born at the top. I will show you several of the lessons at work in my own climb (especially those which blindsided me). I'll also point out some turnings I took without which this book would never have happened. Passages like this are identified by the above pathway symbol. They show you what I am passionate about and give you a sense of my journey. I hope this helps you feel confident about which of my insights are relevant to you, and which you can leave aside.

Discovering how to survive at high corporate altitudes drives Part Two of this book. The result is to expose a pattern which provokes an explosion of questions. Those questions drive Part Three. Some of them are unavoidably personal. For example, I don't assume that 'up' is right or better. Elites are garlanded with prizes for which many have worked very hard. It's natural for them, and maybe us, to assume that what they have is the best life has to offer.

The questions *why do you want what you want?* and *do you really want it?* are disquieting and may seem unnecessary, but will prove essential to understanding power without losing your soul. I can't answer them for you, but I can try to answer them as honestly as possible for myself. If you follow the pathway sections of this book into Part Three, expect to encounter surprises. I did.

Since I was a teenager I've devoured thrillers. It's a kick to know that there are only a few pages of a book left, and in that space the plot to which you have been glued for the past hundred or more will be turned upside down. As I worked on the final pages of *Elites* it was gobsmacking to me to walk into a twist in the meaning of my own life. Most of my adult life I have sought success, thinking that it was some elusive cocktail of money, achievement, power or praise. After writing Part Three I believe that all the time I was actually looking for something else. As it should be in a thriller, the answer was something unseen, yet in plain view.

'Up' is a very short word. In trying to understand it I had help. I've borrowed from brilliant minds, but if you want you can skip to page 32 and come back to this book's intellectual roots later. Pierre Bourdieu and Norbert Elias were two sharp-eyed detectives of ideas from the last century who hungered to understand the complex ways we humans are with each other. They were fascinated by social distinction. As sociologists, they wanted to understand how we create a social landscape with varying levels of prestige; how and why eating with some utensils rather than others, going to this particular college or doing that work comes – in particular places and at particular times – to earn the doer respect. In other words, how we create 'up'.

In slicing this reality open they found the idea of *habitus* helpful. *Habitus* is the only academic word in this book, and it only occurs in this section. It names the way the world shows up for each of us as a result of what we do and where we hang out, and what we have done and where we have hung out in the past. The word 'mindset' is close, but for a closer analogy think of the browser which you use to roam the internet. You don't 'see' the internet directly: your browser makes it show up for you in an intelligible form. Your browser adapts to you, so it's personal; but it's also social; made and re-made by all of us without thinking about it.

Habitus is a browser which is updating in the background all the time, responding to our choices and regardless of them. If we didn't have it, the infinite possibilities in our world would appear as chaos.

Habitus does its heavy lifting by making certain realities and possible actions *obvious*. Here is one of Bourdieu's most famous quotations about *habitus*. He takes the example of the French royal court, concerning who should bow first:

> When you read, in Saint-Simon, about the quarrel of hats (who should bow first), if you were not born in a court society, if you do not possess the *habitus* of a person of the court, if the structures of the game are not also in your mind, the quarrel will seem futile and ridiculous to you. If, on the other hand, your mind is structured

according to the structures of the world in which you play, everything will seem obvious and the question of knowing if the game 'is worth the candle' will not even be asked[1].

Neither Bourdieu nor Elias were snobs. They didn't fawn over the rich and powerful – quite the opposite. In the same spirit, to crack the mystery of today's elites, we will turn to research which Elias led in an English working- and lower middle-class setting in the 1950s (*see page 145 et seq*).

Our society is not showy in the same way as a royal court. Of course, the powerful tend to wear more expensive clothes (even if they are jeans) but we know that someone in a scruffy top and trainers could be a millionaire. So in Part Two of this book we will study those at the top and those who work closely with them primarily by their *habitus*: not by how they show up in the world (what they wear, how they speak, what qualifications they have) but by how the world shows up for them; what strikes them as *obvious*.

This book is about courts of a different kind: temples of power and excellence erected on the meritocratic pillars of merit, hard work and fairness. Another key principle is transparency, so modern courts are often full of glass. People don't bow or scrape, but headhunters are one kind of gatekeeper who inhabit these courts, deciding whether a door which you approach stays closed or opens. I spent eighteen years as one of these gatekeepers. To finish this section, I will tell you about when I decided to pack it in.

---

1   *Practical Reason: On The Theory of Action*, Pierre Bourdieu, Polity Press, Cambridge UK (1998)

Scene: a November morning in Mumbai, 2006. My years as a headhunter had been intensely interesting and rewarding, and the challenges still got me buzzing. But without stepping off that frantic treadmill, I would never have stumbled upon the work of Bourdieu or Elias. I wouldn't have been able to imagine this book, let alone write it.

I was in Mumbai as part of a week-long learning experience organised by the social change enterprise, Leaders' Quest. Leaders' Quest also organised trips to China, a country which I have never visited (beyond my birthplace, Hong Kong). I chose Mumbai because it wasn't China. China felt too close and oppressive.

Therapy does not help me to explain why. I was the first child of two teachers, an English father and a Chinese mother. I fulfilled parental ambitions which took me from an ordinary schooling in Hong Kong to scholarships at Cambridge and Harvard. But I rejected out of hand the disappointment which my parents voiced when I became engaged to someone from a family without university credentials. Equally decisively, I binned those parts of my Chinese heritage which I could not cook or eat. Instead I chose to understand more about India, part of a subcontinent which has played such a significant part in forming contemporary British identity.

It's early, probably before 8am, when we pile out of a minibus on a Mumbai corner. We're (mostly) British executives. This morning a handful of us have opted to meet migrant construction workers who live on the streets. Many of them are women, wiry and strong. Some climb scaffolding with babies on their backs. They are curious, but the city is coming to life and they have jobs to get on with – jobs like getting food, staying alive and trying to live another day. They have these jobs, but today they don't yet have work.

Helped by a translator from a Leaders' Quest local partner, the women ask us what we are doing here. We ask them the same thing. We repeat the encounter three times in different places. By 10.30am the sun is giving us its full tropical attention. We find that we have lived a biblical lesson in the flesh. These workers are hired by the day. The later in the morning we meet them, the more likely that they will finish the day without money for food.

Everyone who took part in that week-long Quest had individual, contrasting experiences. The women in Mumbai changed me. I went back to my job as deputy chairman of a London headhunting firm thinking: here I sit, while so many billions of people cope with so much insecurity every day. If I, decked out in financial, educational and social advantages, can't face the insecurity as I approach fifty of saying goodbye to a monthly salary and exploring what else might be possible, I should be taken out and shot. I resigned the following summer. This book's journey had started.

PART TWO

THE
SENIOR EXECUTIVE'S
SURVIVAL GUIDE

(Lessons for climbing
to the top)

Part Two

The
Senior Executive's
Survival Guide

Three lessons about reality

THREE STRANGERS – A DIRECTOR, an ambitious twenty-five-year-old and an office cleaner – spill out of the same lift at 7.15 one morning. The twenty-five-year-old is a guy, the other two are women. As the doors open on the twentieth floor of an office block, we might think they see the same thing: the deserted reception of the bank where all of them work. But they don't.

The cleaner and the director both notice a coffee spill on the floor, which the twenty-five-year-old misses. The director sees a flickering swathe of green digits behind the desk (stocks are falling and the screen is showing the Chinese market), but the twenty-five-year-old fixes on a half-eaten bowl of cereal in the waiting area. He left it there while he took a cigarette break; he hadn't expected anyone important in the office before 8am.

Reality shows up for them already interpreted according to their social position. It's also pre-loaded with impulses to act. Before the lift doors are fully open, the director is reaching for her encrypted smartphone, the twenty-five-year-old is wiping milk from his upper lip and the cleaner has gripped her mop: their bodies are already in motion in socially appropriate ways. They are not robots. The director could choose to reach for the mop. But none of us starts from a neutral place: some things are already obvious, and what's obvious depends on our social position.

We need to start here because understanding elites involves explaining magic tricks. We hint at magic when we use words like 'star quality' or 'charisma'. To stand any chance of succeeding, we need to grasp that every magic trick starts before the audience thinks it starts. It's vital to go back, way before the bit where the band strikes up some chords and a wizard captures our attention. We have to start with what is too obvious to discuss – lessons about reality. Here are three.

THE FIRST LESSON

MORE BEATS LESS

Do more

Achieve more

Say more

Be more

We learn the first lesson of reality counting sweets: more beats less. $2 + 2 = 4$ but $2 + 2 + 1 = 5$, and five sweets are better than four. If you are a muggle, this lesson will last you from infancy to dotage, from junior muggle to – if you choose to become one – wizard.

As I grew up and became professional I learned counting concepts such as 'cost benefit analysis', 'discounted cash flow' and 'quality-adjusted life years'. Counting turns out to be powerful. If the benefits are more than the costs, then sometimes good people are removed from their homes and airports get new runways. If your quality-adjusted life years are insufficient, it may be the time to type 'funeral services' into your search bar.

Here's the tune once again: more beats less. Scrape some more flesh off the coconut. Squeeze some more cash out of the business. Demand some extra bonus. £246,000 is more than £240,000. $2 + 2 + 1 + 0.7$ is nearly 6. Every little helps. As we learn these lessons, we're learning a bigger lesson: not just how to count, but *who* counts – the person with more achievements. After all, we are talking about meritocratic workplaces.

In order to climb, muggles write down their achievements in a CV or résumé. More achievements lead to new opportunities which lead to more achievements. 'Achieved top-performing region three years in a row.' 'Rolled out diversity training with 92 per cent attendance at reduced cost.' More is better: every little helps.

'More is better' thinking leads to backbreaking toil and

lengthy presentations. Aspirant muggles work more hours, review more data and expound more arguments, in no doubt that they are advancing their cause. I was the same. I ran that race, got the T-shirt and got ready to run a longer race.

But one day in my twenties I happened to be the junior note-taker when a wizard demonstrated that 'more is better' is only true in muggle reality. To think that way is not becoming to people at the top. What's obvious to a wizard is that less is often better.

Four muggles (I was the most junior) arrived to meet one of the wizards in the government department where I worked. My colleagues were senior muggles – what we call in this book 'muggle crust'. They had risen far. They dealt with wizards daily. They were under the wizard's command, but disagreed with him on an important subject. They set out to change his mind.

The senior muggles had prepared meticulously. That was the muggle crust thing to do. The more preparation, the more arguments, the better. They stacked argument after argument in their armoury. Their case was impressive. They were confident, and had good reason to be.

When the day came the wizard's patience was exemplary. Ranged against him were something like nine carefully constructed arguments. My job was to take notes but the wizard scribbled his own in a large notebook. He reviewed them before congratulating my colleagues. Their arguments were 'weighty', 'impressive' and 'difficult to rebut'. The muggle crust began to smile.

The wizard showed off his mastery of each of the arguments, picking out many perceptive details. How we all beamed when he singled out one of the arguments as conclusive, stronger than all the others.

The rest of the meeting was a massacre. The wizard slaughtered that argument (in fact the weakest), leaving it in shreds on the floor. But we had been too busy smiling to dispute the suggestion that this was our strongest argument, so the meeting was over. The muggles would have been better off sticking to their two strongest arguments. This time, as if by magic, the sum total of 2 + 2 + 1 + 0.7 proved to be zero.

It seemed that above the world I understood – the muggle world – there was another, more powerful world; a wizard world, with different rules. I decided to keep my eyes peeled.

I left government work to become a headhunter. Headhunters (executive search consultants) are recruiters who hang around top-level selection processes. I became a midwife to the birth of many wizards. In order to do this, I had to immerse myself in CVs. CVs demonstrate precisely how 'more is better' turns into its opposite when you become a wizard.

To rise, muggles must accumulate many achievements. Following this lesson, muggle crust CVs frequently stretch to four or five pages. *But (first practical way to spot a wizard) no wizard may have a CV longer than one and a half pages. You show me someone with a longer CV, and I'll show you someone who isn't a wizard.*

In fact, the higher a wizard rises, the more her CV shrinks, in line with the (wizard) rule that less is better. The CV of a really top wizard is never more than half a page. Eventually they stop having CVs and have Wikipedia entries and media interviews.

We've started with a clue; a full definition will come. Ripping pages from your current CV won't endow you with magic powers. But it is a handy tip. Remembering that the clue needs to be true of Bezos, Atwood and Lamar on page 24, let's see how it works.

Let Quentin Tarantino be our guide. Take a look at his entry in Wikipedia. Here is what it says about his career until his first hit. Behold a wizard in the making: picture how during the 1980s his résumé gradually gets longer and longer until, soon after *Reservoir Dogs*, it begins to shrink.

At 14 years old, Tarantino wrote one of his earliest works, a screenplay called *Captain Peachfuzz and the Anchovy Bandit*, based on Hal Needham's 1977 film *Smokey and the Bandit* starring Burt Reynolds. The summer after his fifteenth birthday, Tarantino was grounded by his mother for shoplifting Elmore Leonard's novel *The Switch* from Kmart. He was allowed to leave only to attend the Torrance Community Theater, where he participated in such plays as *Two Plus Two Makes Sex* and *Romeo and Juliet*.

At about fifteen, Tarantino dropped out of Narbonne High School in Harbor City, Los Angeles. He then worked as an usher at a porn theatre in Torrance, called the Pussycat Theatre.

Later, Tarantino attended acting classes at the James Best Theatre Company, where he met several of his eventual collaborators. While at James Best, Tarantino also met Craig Hamann, with whom he later collaborated to produce *My Best Friend's Birthday*.

Throughout the 1980s, Tarantino worked a number of jobs. He spent time as a recruiter in the aerospace industry, and for five years, he worked at Video Archives, a video store in Manhattan Beach, California. Former *Buffy the Vampire Slayer* actor Danny Strong described Tarantino as 'such a movie buff. He had so much knowledge of films that he would try to get people to watch really cool movies.'

After Tarantino met Lawrence Bender at a Hollywood party, Bender encouraged him to write a screenplay. His first attempted script, which he described as a 'straight 70s exploitation action movie' was never published and was abandoned soon after. Tarantino co-wrote and directed his first movie, *My Best Friend's Birthday*, in 1987. The final reel of the film was almost completely destroyed in a lab fire that occurred during editing, but its screenplay later formed the basis for *True Romance*.

In 1986, Tarantino got his first Hollywood job, working with Roger Avary as production assistants on Dolph Lundgren's exercise video, *Maximum Potential*.

The following year, he played an Elvis impersonator in 'Sophia's Wedding: Part 1', an episode in the fourth season of *The Golden Girls*, which was broadcast on November 19, 1988.

Tarantino received his first paid writing assignment in the early 1990s when Robert Kurtzman hired him to write the script for *From Dusk Till Dawn*.

In January 1992, Tarantino's neo-noir crime thriller *Reservoir Dogs* – which he wrote, directed and acted in as Mr Brown – was screened at the Sundance Film

Festival. It was an immediate hit, with the film receiving a positive response from critics. The dialogue-driven heist movie set the tone for Tarantino's later films. He wrote the script for the film in three-and-a-half weeks.

(downloaded 19 May, 2019)

My CV tells you that I'm muggle crust. To start with, it's two pages. I can earn money cutting CVs, but cutting mine to a page and a half would feel like amputating an arm or a leg. There's a touch over one page for my executive work, a bit under half a page for charities and boards (including achievements) and a bit under half a page for writing, qualifications and education.

For six years I chaired the Refugee Council, then Britain's largest refugee charity. I was a wizard in the specific world of refugee care – and in that world, my CV was half a page. If I was speaking at your conference, you didn't want more than that: sending two pages would have looked odd.

To see how beautifully these lessons of reality work in the muggle-wizard economy, we need to notice one more thing. Think again about the muggle crust, just below the wizards.

These senior muggles have succeeded greatly. Under their direction the world keeps turning.

Only two kinds of visitor regularly enter wizard space: cleaners, personal trainers, help-desk technicians and the like (I call them 'artisans'), and the muggle crust. They do their jobs: in the case of the muggle crust that might be presenting a report, arguing for a new strategy or being blamed for a cock-up. Then they have to be returned where they belong.

With artisans, this is easy. They can pop in and out of wizard space all day long with no special badging: no wizard will mistake a personal trainer for one of themselves. With the muggle crust it's different. They are experienced professionals, tough and smart. The muggle-wizard boundary would break down unless the muggle crust gain traits which, without their knowing, spill the beans on who they are. Wizards need sticky labels on muggle-crust backs which the muggle crust don't know are there. These muggle badges say, 'I'm handy to have around but don't belong: please send me home after use'.

Long CVs are a drop-dead muggle badge. 'More is better' thinking is intangible but works just as well. No one gets as far as the muggle crust without injecting weekly the first lesson of reality: 'more is better' becomes part of them. To stand out as a muggle, I must get up early, do more, say more, achieve more and be more. And the fact that I think like this – that I look puzzled when a wizard flicks through my board presentation and says, 'Cut it in half' – stamps me as a muggle through and through.

What all this accomplishes is that much of the daily turning of the world is in the hands of an executive caste (the muggle crust) whose lifeblood is over-achievement. Handily for the wizard class, this generates more and more and more – more material advances and more profits. If the wizards feel generous, some of it may trickle down.

And because what produces this abundance also badges the muggle crust, it's easy for wizards to fling wide the doors to their clubs, boardrooms and golf courses. They can be as appreciative and hospitable as may take their fancy. They can do all this and be certain that, come the end of the task at hand, they will know who belongs and who doesn't.

The best trick is that muggle formation can make even ambitious members want to stay in the muggle crust of their own free will. To them the wizard world is weird: they'd rather be home of an evening. This we will explore later on.

THE SECOND LESSON

THE RATIONAL ISN'T PERSONAL

Focus

Think

Act

Leave your personality
at the door

ALL THREE OF THE INDIVIDUALS who step out of the lift onto the bank's twentieth floor (*see page 37*) walk into worlds in which something isn't right. For the cleaner and the director it's a coffee spill on the floor, but let's focus on the twenty-five-year-old.

He is a junior muggle who has inherited responsibility for a series of loans which the bank has made over ten years. The loans are meant to be secured in a way which protects the bank even if the borrower goes under. They have been rolled over several times, each time with many pages of repetitive paperwork. But this young man has read every version of every page (more is better) and spotted something. In fact, the bank isn't protected. What he has discovered is a multi-million dollar headache rather than a disaster, but the situation is embarrassing. He has come in early to find the best way to fix it. At a meeting later that morning he wants to report a solution as well as the problem. If the way he thinks through the legal and financial complexities proves to be robust, his career will have lift-off.

The director was in this position fifteen years ago. She is muggle crust. Her thinking has been kept sharp by more challenges than she can count, each one nastier and messier than the last. She will need all her rational skills today because, unexpectedly, the Chinese market is a car crash. Don't worry, like the best of the muggle crust she will be at her best today. She will be like a surgeon in A&E.

Someone arrives from a car accident with a crushed pelvis. Assess the situation calmly. Ensure life-support. Get imaging of the damage. Assemble the theatre team. Depersonalise. Take off jewellery and put on gowns. Scrub, disinfect and cut the patient open – rationally.

The muggle crust have been picked for being smarter, faster, more rational than average. They solve crises calmly. They dial down emotions, assess the situation, assemble the team, take off personalities and focus intensely on roles. They cut the problem open and solve it rationally. If a retractor is needed, which member of the team hands it to the surgeon doesn't matter. Today in a tumbling market the director's carefully honed thinking will keep the bank's losses to a fraction of what they might have been, and earn her a promotion to start attending the top executive committee. There is no entry for wizard in the senior executive handbook, but that's what she is being tried out for.

Twelve months further on, she receives feedback from her boss (a wizard) and 'peers' (muggle crust but senior to her), collected anonymously as part of a systematic human resources exercise. Her intellect is mostly well-rated, although one comment adds that 'she's not as smart as she thinks she is'. But it's the descriptions of her *personality* as 'arrogant', 'pushy' and 'cuts across colleagues' which hurt and feel deeply untrue.

The director's friends are mystified – the person they know is quiet, even shy. More to the point, she always leaves her personality out of work meetings. She tackles problems rationally. True, she has felt some need to produce more than others in order to qualify as their equal (more is better), but that is humility rather than arrogance. Faced with new responsibilities, she has doubled down on that philosophy. Her contributions are always to the point, sometimes alerting the group to a short-cut to an unnoticed solution. To summarise: she started her career where the twenty-five-year-old is today. To reach the muggle crust she has expanded those rational talents with surgical precision. Yet her boss, one of her keen admirers, now wonders whether she has less potential than he had first thought. This member of the muggle crust may have reached her peak. She may not be cut out to be a wizard.

From a wizard point of view, her mistake is clear. Believing through and through that the rational isn't personal, she is convinced that it makes no difference who hands the retractor to the surgeon, if a retractor is needed. On top of this, she needs to earn her place, and more is better. But in any wizard grouping it always makes a difference who does what. If the new kid on the block beats the others irritatingly often, the group's other members have a choice between two explanations. Either the newbie is smarter than they are or she has a pushy personality. This subconscious choice is a no-brainer: the rational turns into the personal.

Incidentally, had she taken the opposite tactic of saying only a few things, the lesson would have been the same. Her occasional suggestions might have passed unnoticed, until stolen (without acknowledgement) by one of her senior colleagues later in the discussion. There is no purely rational solution to the dilemma. In the wizard world, it always matters who is offering the retractor.

If the director does not find a way through, she will have hit a glass ceiling. Something is blocking her which rationality cannot unblock. If the twenty-five-year-old rises far enough, he will hit it too, although the glass is thicker for the woman – while she gets called arrogant, he might be thought of as acceptably ambitious. Still, he won't become a wizard without learning from our second lesson.

When we looked at how 'more is better' is true for muggles but not for wizards, we saw that this flip does two things for the muggle-wizard economy. First off, wizards reap the rewards of an ever more productive and profitable turning of the world run by a muggle crust which cannot rest (more is better). Second, to do their job the muggle crust can roam freely in wizard spaces, because their way of thinking stamps them as temporary visitors (they are badged in a way they cannot see).

What does rationality being impersonal for muggles but not for wizards achieve? The twenty-five-year-old will not rise as a muggle without honing his objective thinking, stripping out personal irrelevancies. So a rich concentration of perceptive, unemotional, rational faculties builds up in the muggle crust, solving many problems in the world and creating progress. This also functions as a problem filter: most rationally soluble problems are dealt with before they trouble wizards. Wizard-level problems need to be 'solved' with other tricks. And, because wizard thinking is always personal, objective rationality also functions as a muggle badge. In the wizard world, it always matters who offers the solution.

To enter a senior group successfully – to get a proper listening when what you have to say is unfamiliar or difficult – is tricky, whether your entrance is permanent or just for a specific task. When it goes wrong you want the ground to swallow you up. I remember times like that.

One evening I turned up as a headhunter at the chamber of a local council alone, wet and late. The council's chief executive was retiring and a committee of elected councillors were interviewing search firms in order to choose his successor. My train was delayed, rain started, there were no taxis and I had no umbrella. When I found the main entrance after 7pm, the council members had already been waiting ten minutes beyond my appointed time. The front entrance was locked. Finding the back way in took forever.

The retiring chief executive sat to one side. Everybody wanted to be home: certainly I did. The councillors weren't going to give the job to me in these circumstances. *I* wouldn't have done!

But they sat politely through my presentation and then asked questions. One was what role should the outgoing chief executive play in selecting his successor, a subject on which I and my firm had strong views. 'Well, they're not going to give me the work anyway,' I thought as I turned to face the chief executive. He had been silent throughout the process. I wiped drips from my spectacles and named several important contributions which he could make to a successful process, but selecting candidates – no. That should happen with him outside the room.

I got home and dried off. The next morning we got the work. The leader of the council explained, 'You were the only firm we saw with the courage to tell the chief executive no'. It turned out that the chief executive had dominated the council for years. The councillors were terrified that he would stop them choosing someone from a different mould. This was a situation in which only one firm offered the councillors the specific retractor they needed. So sometimes – not often – having the right answer is enough. More useful to know is that you can get through that awful not-belonging feeling and survive.

THE THIRD LESSON

REALITY IS SIMPLE

Things exist or they don't

WITH *MORE BEATS LESS* and the idea that *rationality isn't personal*, progressing from junior muggle into the muggle crust and then becoming a wizard involved a single mental flip. Now we'll look at a triple flip.

Take an everyday task: changing a nappy, painting a wall or serving six customers at a restaurant table. At first it looks straightforward. But the novice has no clue about the complications which appear out of nowhere. Skill and experience make pitfalls vanish. So every junior muggle's first steps in the workplace teach a flip: reality looks simple but is, in fact, complicated.

But becoming steeped in complexity doesn't get you into the muggle crust. If our twenty-five-year-old comes to love detail and the relationship becomes permanent, he will stay a technical expert or a middle manager. To break into the muggle crust he will have to master a second flip. New simplicities must be announced. They sound like this: cash is king; the customer is always right; move fast and break things. So the pumpkin which turned into Cinderella's carriage is a pumpkin once more – if you have the eyes to see.

But to become a wizard needs a third flip. Reality becomes complex again, worse than before. The pumpkin turns out to be *volatile, uncertain, complex and ambiguous* (as they like to say in business schools).

An example: speech. We may think that words are either spoken or not, but wizards go 'off the record': 'What I'm about to say I will only say if we both agree that I never said it. Do you agree?' If both parties play ball, were the words said or not?

Going 'off the record' isn't a theoretical amusement. It's a real-world competence which fixes deals, gets people jobs, moves cash and keeps secrets secret – or blows them out of the water.

In business nothing is more real than money, so let's watch how our twenty-five-year-old's thinking somersaults. Back when he was a student, money was simple (and he never had enough of it). But to get to wear his bank's 10k finisher T-shirt, he had to learn that finance was complicated. To join the muggle crust, he'll have to learn how to reduce a complex aircraft financing deal to three key points. He will have come a long way, but if it's the top he wants, there's one more flip to come.

I'm H, a headhunter paid by the Department of Health in London. They are creating a big new national role. I'm talking to C, a candidate. The job interviews are finished: the Department wants C – badly. There's no-one else with C's mix of experience, and he knows that. He's interested – it will be a career-defining, big-wizard job, unless he takes it in circumstances which set him up to fail. Then it will be career-defining in a bad way. I don't remember the exact words but here are the thoughts:

H: There won't be another opportunity in your lifetime or mine to shape the future of healthcare like this, in a role which has never existed before. It's yours. The department wants you.

C: I hear you. But Tony [Blair, the Prime Minister] made another speech. So many new-fangled trusts licensed in a few months. It may not be possible. The civil servants swear it's all on track, they've been hard at it for months. Maybe, but it could be a train smash. This is so different to anything the department has planned before. If I take the job and I inherit crap, I'll end up with the blame.

(Silence.)

H: Can I talk off the record?

C: Of course.

H: Meaning you never got what I'm about to say from me.

C: Yes.

H: Like you, I think the Department isn't remotely ready. But how about taking the job on condition that the minute you sign, you appoint independent consultants to assess in a week or two the readiness of the department's preparations. If it's all good, fine. If there's a problem, you can say Tony's timetable has to change.

Which is what C proposed and the department agreed. Reportedly, management consulting firm McKinsey went on to bill more than £20 million for follow-on work as a result of being in on the birth of NHS foundation trusts.

The three flips benefit wizards like this. On their behalf, the muggle crust manage complicated operations but report back in crisp simplicities. That's like having a top-notch accountant or doctor who spares you gobbledygook. Wizards can use the energy which this saves to do magically complicated things which put the accountant or doctor firmly in their place.

However, having three flips is confusing. If someone's grasp of reality seems simple, are they a novice or muggle crust? If it's complicated, are they a junior muggle or a wizard? So, *reality is simple* isn't the best muggle badge. However, we have plenty of badges to be getting on with.

As we finish with reality and turn to what wizards know about relationships, let's lighten the mood and explain the third lesson in terms of cats.

Start here. Reality is simple: a cat exists or it does not. Agreed?

Damn, physicist Erwin Schrödinger discovers his famous paradox. He thinks about a cat sealed in a box with a phial of poison gas (charming). The release of the gas is triggered randomly by radioactive decay. Reality is now complex: the cat is now both dead and alive until the box is opened. Look, this is physics, not made-up stuff!

The muggle crust wrestle with this mess until simplicity is restored. They think 'strategically'. For example, simply by dispatching enough cats in enough boxes (how many depends on how far we have to send them and the rate of radioactive decay), we can guarantee the delivery of a live cat with 99 per cent probability. Hurrah! We look forward to becoming CEO of Uber Cat.

Wizard insight thrusts us back into a horrendous mess by noticing that our logistics business may be guilty of species genocide, complete with lethal gas. The Nuremberg trials return, but with cats.

Three lessons about relationships

THE NEXT THREE LESSONS are about relationships. Before we move on, let's emphasise a pattern which will deepen in the pages to come. What kinds of things are these 'lessons'?

Take another look at the chapter headings on the Contents page. I've highlighted ten lessons which need to be, or become, obvious to any muggle who wants to reach the muggle crust. Our twenty-five-year-old won't get to where the director is unless these things become not only obvious but profoundly ingrained. What this book explores is the idea that the director will not make it into the wizardry without new things becoming obvious. The first two lessons flipped to their opposites, but the third did something more complicated.

When a lesson 'flips', the previous teaching wasn't wrong. The twenty-five-year-old won't climb high unless he inhales deeply lessons which the director, if she wants to become a wizard, now needs to flip. Since the next lessons are about relationships, we will see that 'flipping' involves much more than mental tricks. Lesson two warned us: the journey we're on is personal.

THE FOURTH LESSON

BE TRANSPARENT

Stick to the truth
Don't conceal

ON 5 AUGUST 2010, 700,000 tonnes of rock caved in on top of 33 miners working in the Atacama desert, several kilometres from the mine entrance and almost a kilometre underground. First Chile, then the world, was gripped. A global rescue effort was led by André Sougarret, a top engineer from the Chilean state mining company, as well as Chilean mining minister Laurence Golborne.

On the seventeenth day a drill bit returned to the surface with a handwritten message, 'We are alive in the refuge, the 33'. Until then it had been odds on that the men had died, or would die, unfound. Even after this miraculous message, the unpredictable, unstable terrain meant that the chances of drilling an escape route accurately enough in time were less than 1 in 80.

From the beginning, Golborne and Sougarret were transparent about the awful odds. There was to be no false hope or cruel deception. They declared their objective to be to bring the men home, dead or alive; even this was against the odds. But they would give the near-impossible their best, most honest effort.

We have all known wretched confusion and hopelessness. In order to keep going rather than turn into jelly, who hasn't clung fiercely to a moral compass? I imagine Sougarret felt like that. Confronting a 'to do' list of impossibles with millions watching, 'be transparent' would have stood out as do-able, honourable and reassuring. Good news he couldn't promise, but honest news and every ounce of effort he could.

Climbing as a muggle throws up regular honesty

challenges. Poor performance has to be reviewed, bad news given to bosses and clients, deadlines revised and mistakes owned up to. While a few make their way to the top apparently dodging bullet after bullet, most of the muggle crust have learned to give and receive tough messages. In decision after decision over sixty-nine long days, Sougarret proved that he was tough, decisive and straight.

However, *reality isn't simple.* As the rescue unfolded, it tested Sougarret – without question a hero – deeply: in our terms, was he muggle crust or wizard?

Jonathan Franklin is an award-winning international journalist who lives in Chile. The only journalist with access inside the rescue perimeter, he reported on the rescue daily for media around the world, making detailed notes. Two events from his subsequent book[2] show how Sougarret's commitment to transparency buckled under the pressure of events.

After the miners had been found, a communication tube was the first priority. The 33 knew that for none of them was survival assured. The drill jockeys would have to be incredibly lucky to beat the odds mentioned earlier. The layers of rock groaned and moved regularly. But still, to receive clean water, food, medicines and messages through a communication tube the diameter of just a fist was pure heaven.

Some weeks later, still underground, the 33 revolted in anger. Without anyone being told, family letters were being opened before being passed down. The miners had worked this out from inconsistencies in the messages. What was happening was that contraband drugs and bad news were

---

2   *The 33*, Transworld Publishers, 2011

removed from the letters, on professional advice (from a psychologist) but on Sougarret's authority. Hundreds of letters were not passed on at all. The arrangement was the opposite of transparent. The miners were furious. The psychologist was replaced. From then on, the miners got their mail, and drugs if they were that way inclined, without interference.

As the moment approached when it was hoped to bring the men to the surface one at a time in a narrow capsule, there was a global media frenzy. A worldwide audience exceeding one billion – naturally including the men's families and friends – bit their nails watching a live video feed from the refuge. With a day to go, a rockfall severed the communication link which carried the video and threatened to abort the whole rescue. Sougarret decided to say nothing. He fooled the whole world with a re-run of the video feed from 24 hours previously, while the team worked flat-out (and at considerable risk) to retrieve the situation. When connection was restored, someone remembered just in time to ask the remaining miners to move outside the camera angle, so they could cut from lie back to truth without a billion viewers noticing.

Reality is not simple. For a wizard, transparency is not always the answer. In fact, disclosure is one of the most advanced wizard arts. For good or ill, Sougarret was (or became) a wizard.

The achievement of all the rescuers is mind-blowing. These two examples of deception can't touch the achievement of Sougarret and his colleagues: on the contrary, we see how morally complicated real leadership gets. And we begin to sense why all muggle crust do not want to become wizards.

Being transparent is the first job of a glass ceiling. The term 'glass ceiling' began to be used in the 1970s to describe a transparent, invisible barrier which limits the rise to the very top mainly of women and people of colour. The barrier is transparent in both directions. Those below see nothing obstructing their rise as high as their effort, talent and a bit of luck will take them; neither do those above, who walk on a glass floor. One way of thinking about The Senior Executive's Survival Guide is that it aims to explain why meritocracies produce glass ceilings. I prefer to talk about wizards and muggles because what's happening, which is a bit magical, is personal and happens inside our heads, whatever our gender, race or education. A glass ceiling appears to be impersonal, something external, built by someone else when we weren't looking.

But the idea of a glass ceiling can help tease out the implications of scale. If there was a glass dome over most of our heads, we would see maintenance crews out and about every day. Our sky would always have orange dots in it, climbing girders and manoeuvring replacement panes. Keeping the glass ceiling going would be a big-bucks business. To keep a glass ceiling going inside all of our heads isn't any easier a task, but where are the maintenance crews? Where's the money flow? For ceiling-building to be going on under our noses without our noticing would be quite a trick.

A good chunk of the trick is called business schools, which have spread their influence widely. In addition to master's degrees, business and management are the top undergraduate subjects in Britain and America. Factor in the role which such schools played in elevating shareholder value to become the sole goal of business, and you are talking about a huge level of societal influence. Some schools and some professors take a very different approach, but they are in the minority.

One of the most elite schools is Harvard, which publishes a magazine with a very wide senior readership (the *Harvard Business Review*). Let's watch it do some ceiling-building in the aftermath of the Chilean mine rescue.

Three years after the mine collapse the magazine published an article by three Harvard academics called 'Leadership Lessons from The Chilean Mine Rescue'[3]. The authors picked out three lessons to learn from Sougarret and his colleagues. All three lessons involved top leaders perceiving situations especially well and then being very clever. (Coincidentally, perceiving situations especially well and being very clever are the qualities on which research academics pride themselves.)

None of the moral messiness described above – and many other examples are available, including from the leadership ups and downs that happened underground, where 33 men made do on one teaspoon each of tuna a day – makes it into the case study. The article is written for aspiring muggles and the muggle crust. It tells them that reaching the summit is like climbing a tricky rational mountain in bright sunlight: complicated but transparent. *But here is the glass ceiling being*

---

3   Rashid, Edmondson and Leonard, *Harvard Business Review*, July-August 2013

built in front of us. The obstacle is the idea that the game doesn't change. The obstacle is doubling down on the hard work and smart thinking that got you this far. The obstacle is constructed in your mind: it's the idea that there is no obstacle.

From the wizard point of view – looking down from above the glass ceiling – 'be transparent' is a riot. First, the saving in wizard energy and anxiety from being able to count on honesty and transparency from your lieutenants is enough to power several cities. Second, the ambitious muggle crust become birds-on-speed, flying harder and harder into the glass ceiling (because they're sure it doesn't exist). This is funny to watch and a ton of work gets done in the process. Third, some of the muggle crust stop, burn out or make different choices. Concealing stuff is yucky. They prefer *wysiwyg* (what you see is what you get). In fact, *wysiwyg* is one of the best muggle badges, because wizards always have a little something up their sleeves: it's their job.

THE FIFTH LESSON

DEFER TO BOSSES AND CLIENTS

Be a devoted nobody

THE TRUTH ABOUT BIG SHOTS is that they lap up an astonishing amount of deference. Payment can be by cash or card, by job titles and pay packages or by dedicated meeting rooms with designer coffee cups. But the most common payment is the destruction of large amounts of other people's time, whether in working through the night, endless waiting or voluntary presenteeism.

To grasp the fifth lesson, we need to look more closely at the working relationship between a big shot and you. Let's split the connection into 'the job' and the etiquette. 'The job' is the work you've done and the results you've got. The etiquette is please, thank you and holding the door. To reach the muggle crust and knock on the door of wizardry we need to keep one eye on each.

Crawling is not a good way to go. Crawling involves over-delivering on the job (but only the bits that please, never anything that challenges) while turning up to max the flattery and obsequiousness. The nail in this approach's coffin is that obsequiousness is the muggle badge to beat all muggle badges. Crawling guarantees you life muggle membership. Wizards don't do obsequious. (If you spot a crawler high up in your organisation, you can deduce that the glass ceiling is above them.)

The prospects of success through bullying are better, but not by much. With luck the meritocracy will weed you out (hurrah), but if you do make it into the muggle crust you might go further (boo). Sadly, some wizards are bullies.

The most common meritocratic strategy – the clue is in

the name – is to concentrate on the work and hope it speaks for itself. Etiquette becomes common courtesy (saying 'good morning' to everyone in the same way, not getting close to anyone powerful) because anything more complicated is too hard to get right. This works fine for getting into middle management, but is too colourless (too lacking in 'personal brand') to get you into the crust. Wizards are colourful, they have personality, and the muggle crust show some of that glow.

In the end, deference leads to no glow. The better path is mutual respect served with a splash of confidence and a dash of personality. You can practise mixing this cocktail wherever you are in your career.

Mutual respect means delivering reliably on 'the job', but also includes occasionally challenging your boss or client back. Things to be challenged include ridiculous deadlines or expectations – that's part of insisting that there is a level of respect appropriate to your position, however junior. (If challenging ridiculous deadlines is always a sackable offence, you are in the wrong place, however platinum-plated the selection process you passed in order to get in.)

Etiquette starts with some friendly courtesy to everyone (why not surprise someone – not just more senior colleagues – by holding open a door?) but do it without role-playing a bellboy at The Ritz (obsequiousness). A deeper courtesy is, without being asked, to do some thinking which will save your boss five or ten minutes of their time. It's an appropriate form of respect and, at least some of the time, will be noticed. Mutual respect isn't the same as equal respect: you and your boss are not peers, nor should you pretend to be. Whatever nice gestures you choose to make, do them out of confident strength not weakness: you're not following rules, this is just the kind of person you are.

The trickiest bit is adding the dash of personality. Imagine that you have escorted the CEO of Boeing (definitely a wizard) downstairs, and his chauffeur will drive up in three minutes. You ask, human to human, whether he watched the football at the weekend, or mention a place you particularly enjoyed in Sardinia (because you've done your homework and you know which club he supports, or that he was tweeting from Sardinia a couple of weeks ago). You don't prolong the conversation, because he's busy and you're not a peer: but you are a human. It's like adding Tabasco to a Bloody Mary: the right amount is what the person you're talking to thinks is the right amount, not what suits your taste.

Why bother? Most big shots are bored stiff with the deference and blandness they get from corporate staff. Besides, today's leaders are keen to think of themselves as 'good' with 'ordinary people'. Do it in a way which makes the big shot confident you're not about to embarrass them by asking for a pay rise or starting a ten-minute pub story involving a dachshund, a poodle and an Irish setter, and the chances are you'll get a friendly response however junior you are. More importantly, you will be getting started on a key muggle–wizard relationship skill; one which might in ten years' time get you invited to a dinner party on a yacht. To get that invitation, you will by then have to have a sufficiently important job, but you will also need to be an interesting enough muggle for wizards to dine with, and one who definitely won't embarrass them by thinking one dinner has made you a wizard. That skill is learned by practice.

Instead of flips this lesson is about a gradual, thoughtful rise in the amount of 'you' which becomes part of the day job. Even as a wizard the percentage doesn't have to be very high. While the context of different activities varies, you can be a wizard and be quiet. (Fifty years ago in large parts of the British establishment they had to be – the background noise of power was hushed whispers.) But you can't be a nonentity. If you're a wizard, we are going to tell stories about you. And we like good ones.

One of my favourite muggle-wizard stories is about Henry Kissinger, the brain who ran American foreign policy under President Richard Nixon. Whether or not the story is apocryphal doesn't matter. I've added the word 'muggle': the original was 'aide' or 'staffer'. It's also a great story about the limits of deference.

A muggle has worked hard to deliver a briefing paper which the secretary of state has requested. The following morning, Kissinger calls the muggle in. Without looking up from his desk he asks, 'Is this the best that you can do?' Embarrassed, the muggle takes the paper back and works on it more.

The cycle repeats. Eventually, asked for a third time, 'Is this the best that you can do?', the muggle reaches the limits of her deference. She snaps back, 'Damn you, yes!' At which point the wizard looks up, smiles and says, 'Good. Then I'll read it'.

THE SIXTH LESSON

TAKE RESPONSIBILITY

The buck stops here

To ADVANCE, MUGGLES learn again and again to take on more onerous kinds of responsibility. Some of the experiences will have been painful, but by the time a muggle reaches the crust this sixth lesson is perhaps the most obvious principle of them all. In fact, taking responsibility defines the muggle class.

Junior muggles learn first to take responsibility for their mistakes. (As Donald Trump has proven, it is possible to become a wizard without ever getting to first base as a muggle. However it's only a route to bet on if you're feeling very lucky.)

Next comes being responsible for an activity, an operation, a group of people or an asset – taking care of it, fixing problems, developing it. You have gone a long way if what you are responsible for takes on the trustworthy quality of a stable, resilient platform. Once you have got that, then you can try fancier stuff.

Muggles in the crust do that. They take responsibility for results, for exceeding targets and creating value and delight. And when they see something falling between the cracks of different areas of responsibility, they step up without being asked, nipping problems in the bud. The way the sixth lesson is written into the DNA of the muggle crust helps the world run a lot better. Anyone who has had to extract some service out of an operation in which no one takes responsibility has the scars to prove it. In a bad case (a hospital, for example), a workplace where no one takes responsibility can be dangerous and extremely unpleasant.

That the muggle crust have responsibility in their DNA benefits wizards. First, if hospitals and other complex organisations run well, wizards benefit directly when they need those services. Second, when things go wrong, it's a dream come true for wizards to have beneath them a corps of leaders who own up to their mistakes, take hits for the team and step unhesitatingly into gaps which wizards had failed to spot.

Aspiring muggles learn to be responsible for their actions: wizards do that sometimes, but also practise how to make sure that no responsibility sticks. Aspiring muggles learn how to run activities reliably; wizards do that sometimes, but they also learn how to move fast and break things. By the time they reach the crust, muggles take responsibility for achieving results, in some cases losing their jobs if targets are not met. Wizards do that sometimes, but they also learn to invent targets so magically conceived that all accountability attaches to others. Wizards applaud when muggles step in harm's way to stop things falling down the cracks between different responsibilities – and sometimes they model this behaviour themselves. But at home they practise hard how to create ambiguity and use it, and how to spot falling knives so they don't try to catch them.

Muggles learn to talk the responsibility talk and always to walk the walk. Wizards *always* talk the talk, *often* walk the walk and *sometimes do the complete opposite*. So: this lesson doesn't show a simple flip (more is better), a multiple flip (reality is simple) or a progressive change (defer to bosses and clients). It's more like a little bit of magic: now you see me taking responsibility; now you don't. However, *always* taking responsibility is a reliable muggle badge.

One afternoon I'm in an inner sanctum of the Cabinet Office when a permanent secretary and a panel of other wizards, charged by law with appointing on merit, decide who should fill a top job. For decades, the role has been occupied by a string of white Establishment figures, almost all men. After the interviews, the choice comes down to a white male businessman or a black woman. Both good – equally good, the panel thinks. The decision hangs in the balance. The wizard in charge sums up this way: although the woman is as good as the man, if we pick her, people will think we did it out of political correctness. If we pick the man, we won't have that problem. His colleagues concur. The white man it is.

My job is now to make telephone calls to all the shortlisted candidates, including both of these individuals. But for a moment I'm in an inner corridor of the Cabinet Office thinking, how far can I be from a police officer? Don't I have an offence of gender and racial discrimination to report? But I report nothing. I don't take responsibility. I help hide a 'wizards-only' conversation.

There are some arguments, not particularly good ones, for what I did. (One thing which lots of education buys you is no shortage of reasons for whatever you decide to do.) For what it is worth, some years later I played a part in getting that woman into that job. But it shouldn't have happened that way, and in the meantime I'm part of a cover-up.

Four lessons about advancement

WE HAVE NOW COVERED enough ground to ask a question. Why are there flips and twists? Why isn't the game the same all the way up to the top? To help answer this let me fill a gap. I have been talking about wizards and muggles, and that will remain our focus. But I have left out an entire class.

Let's call the missing group 'artisans', because without freshly made sandwiches or hand-roasted coffee beans delivered to the door, how satisfactory would muggle life be? Not very. Plumbing would also be a challenge. These days muggles respect quality artisan work. However, fraternity has its limits. For instance, muggle parents might enjoy sparky conversation with their daughter's new artisan friend who brought home freshly cut ingredients to cook for dinner. But if he did that because he is a shift worker for HelloFresh, we can expect a different reaction.

Individual artisans may take great pride in their work but taking responsibility in a wider sense is not an organising principle for them in the way it is for muggles. Instead, the most common organising principle of artisan life is survival.

Taking responsibility often involves deferring gratification. It is easier to do if your life sits on a stable platform, when you have time to think and actions have predictable consequences. If instead your life is like a leaf in a gust of wind, reality shows up differently. Suppose that a piece of taking responsibility which really matters to you (maybe buying a child's birthday present) gets dashed by fate (your overdraft rockets up thanks to mistaken charges, but you can't get the bank to put it right before Monday). Life looks different.

In the muggle world, reasonable stability is a condition of life – most of the time it's simply there. Should goldfish spend time wondering what would happen if the sides of their fish tank shattered? No, the organising principle of goldfish life – what makes it interesting to be a goldfish – needs to be something else. A degree of assured survival provides the reliable sides of the muggle fish tank, so for muggles life must be about something else. Until we get to the muggle crust taking responsibility, planning for the future and investing in education works very well.

Take the phrase 'It's not my job'. Its meaning flips in the journey from artisan to junior muggle to muggle crust. It's a truism of artisan life (doing something which isn't your job may get you fired; it certainly won't get you paid) but heresy in the muggle crust.

But now, precisely because the muggle crust is so assiduous and effective about taking responsibility, the world created by their strenuous achievement turns into the fish tank sides for the elite at the top. That's why we should expect the lessons to change. The organising principle of wizard life (magic) must be different from all the sensible behaviour which creates the stable sides of the wizards' tank.

THE SEVENTH LESSON

LEARN STUFF

Everyone should learn stuff
(except managers)

MOST WIZARDS KNOW tons of stuff. Think back to the list on page 24 – Jeff Bezos, Margaret Atwood, Kendrick Lamar. 'Learn stuff' helps muggles climb, except in one area.

Managers easily catch learning rot. The first symptom is arrogance in managing people who know stuff about which the manager hasn't a clue. Managing is itself a skilled art, but we have already pointed to the harm done by business schools alongside the good. Throw in management fads and business hagiographies and you have a lot of learning rot. For most managers, sheer busy-ness and being overwhelmed by the inbox finishes the job. 'Learn stuff' gets crushed into an unrecognisable pea-sized lump called 'don't learn anything which can't be summarised in two paragraphs'.

Putting learning rot aside, the lesson 'learn stuff' doesn't flip or reverse. What changes is what wizards have to learn, and how they learn it.

Here's what I propose an elite – a distinct wizard world – is. We'll unpack the definition and then tease out what it tells wizards to learn and how they need to learn it. For the moment treat the definition as an experiment. Let's play with it a bit and see if it does useful work. Does magic fall into place? Can we see why lessons flip and glass ceilings form? If yes, then we have a useful idea.

Our focus is on meritocratic workplaces, but I believe an elite will form like a skin on top of any group of people doing more or less anything in a sustained way. *An elite is a stranger-free group (a group in which every member either knows, or knows of, every other member), which sees the world in a shared way and which admits new members by group consensus.* The easiest way to get a first idea of the boundaries of an elite is to work out who could message or call whom with a personal request and get a reply, even though the two individuals might not have a direct relationship.

For instance: suppose you work in a large corporation. Certainly the chief executive and her executive committee return each other's messages and calls, including personal requests. Who else is in that group? Your boss, for example? If he approached members of the top team with a personal request, how many would reply? If most of them, he's in; he's a wizard. If not, he isn't.

In some settings the wizard group might be large. I'll guess that in the Catholic church any cardinal will return a phone call from another cardinal, even though they might never have met.

Elites don't have to sit within organisations; what matters is a shared activity: professional football, for instance. We could start with the managers of the top five Premier League clubs and keep testing how far the boundary stretches: who would be able to get a personal email or call returned from most of the group-thus-far? We will add managers, owners, players and journalists: but not *all* managers, *all* owners, *all* players or *all* journalists. Only some will be wizards.

Willingness to respond to a 'personal request' is a handy

cheat; the rigorous test is whether there is deep common ground in how the individuals see the world. So any of the top names in premiership football would return a call from Prince William and *vice versa*, not least because the prince is President of the Football Association. But his immersion in the game would have to be very deep before the footballers counted him as 'one of us'.

The 'stranger-free' bit of being a wizard is like being part of an extended family; between you and any other wizard there is always some connection. When two wizards connect who haven't met before their conversation will zoom in on people, events or institutions in common. Elite boundaries can stretch to knowledge at one remove: if I know I could call a wizard who could tell me about you, that's enough. The important bit is not making the call but knowing that I could: that's enough for you not to be a stranger.

To summarise: wizards are a group with a world and a worldview in common. Wizards may know each other directly or through mutual connections; failing that, both know enough people that either can find out about the other very quickly. An extended family is only a partial analogy. In families worldviews may clash violently, and new members join all the time without general consent.

These are important steps, so let's not rush. Elites form within the context of larger activity groups. The larger group needs to be big enough to include unconnected people (strangers), and the group needs to stick at its activity long enough for some to emerge as better at bits of it than others. Elites can crystallise around different things within the activity, but our focus is meritocratic elites. These crystallise around doing the group activity better.

All of us know far more about meritocratic elites than we may realise. Think of any activity which you have ever tried to take up (perhaps skateboarding, blogging, a kind of cooking or playing a musical instrument) and re-read this section, thinking about the groups you encountered, and how you discovered what counted as good, 'cool', worthy of respect or emulation.

Defining elites is a crucial step, but not as exciting as what we can now explore. How strange to think that knowledge hard-won on school playgrounds might connect to what makes an elite. If it does connect, what magic trick makes us throw that knowledge away when we think of – to return to our previous examples – Bezos, Atwood, Lamar? Or turn the question round: can playgrounds really say anything about star quality and brilliance, when we saw precious little of it when we were growing up?

If the definition is even partly right, it says that wizards need to know two things. First, how to see the world broadly as other wizards do. In particular, most of the things which are obvious to wizards need to become obvious to you. Second, you need to know (or know of) as many other wizards as possible, and to be known (or known of) in return.

It might seem that the easiest way to do both of these things is to absorb them with your mother's milk. Get wizard parents! However, we can't all be Chelsea Clinton, and rejecting all that parents stand for happens a lot. This route also contains a trap. Some of this book's lessons ('take responsibility' is an example) say that wizards have to be able to do what the muggle crust learns, as well as being able to reverse it. Communist China has an excellent word to describe wizard offspring (in China the big wizards are top Party cadres) who know only the wizard stuff and none of the muggle hard grind. The word is 'princelings'.

Most commonly, new wizards are muggles who join by apprenticeship: understudying a senior wizard, being a high-level gofer. This takes time, and only senior wizards are trusted to do the teaching. Having to follow closely a senior wizard keeps the numbers of new joiners down and, if the relationship goes well, builds personal loyalty. In time the senior wizard says, 'This one is worthy', and other wizards trust that judgement. (Of course they'll also keep an eye on what the new wizard gets up to and draw their own conclusions.) Following the senior wizard around, the apprentice gets to meet and be known by other wizards. At the same time, often without thinking or noticing, apprentices learn to find obvious what wizards find obvious.

Apprenticeship opportunities can be shared out in various ways. At the fair end is open competition or enlightened talent management. At the other end is a Hollywood-style meat market in which would-be wizards throw themselves at potential patrons, with possibly alarming consequences. The most enchanted yet patronising approach is arduous discovery Cinderella-style: senior wizards roam the world on a permanent quest, scrutinising all they meet. Once in a while a star is born.

All of this activity is big business. Who would guess that the Cinderella model of wizard recruitment is recommended by the smartest, most intellectually rigorous, global brand in business? Management consulting firm McKinsey is full of super-analytical people who know tons of stuff and whip out thick Powerpoint presentations. It's all about big data, stupid? No, it isn't. It's all about pixie dust: knowing, and being known by, the names who matter most.

As 2000 approached McKinsey invented 'the war for talent'. The idea is that 'talent' is scarce and employers should fight hard for it. What a wizard-friendly idea! In 2018 McKinsey gave that message a big boost. Dominic Barton, McKinsey's global chief, and two co-authors[4] suggested that two per cent of any organisation's employees far outperform the rest. Really? Was McKinsey about to lay off 98 per cent of its own staff? No. The figure which tumbled out of the authors' sleeves was a fantasy. But a key action which the book recommends is the Cinderella model: CEOs should search high and low, 24/7, throughout their kingdoms for the magical few – the candidate-wizards whom only a wizard can recognise. If you work in a large corporation, your talent management system probably looks far less romantic, but it's amazing how prosaic the girders and pipes of a magic factory can look.

If waiting around to be discovered doesn't cut it for you, then this survival guide will try to be your apprentice master. It addresses what wizards need to know and how to make

---

4   Dominic Barton, with Ram Charan and Dennis Carey, *Talent Wins: The New Playbook for Putting People First* (Harvard Business Review Press 2018).

your own pixie dust (how do you get to know, and get known by, the wizards in your world if no one has taken you under their wing?). In Part Three we will go further: challenging the world (why is it this way?); challenging ourselves on what we want for ourselves; and challenging how the system could change.

I spent six years as a wizard within the community in Britain concerned about refugees. I was chair of the country's largest refugee charity, the British Refugee Council, with several hundred staff and more volunteers. People knew me or could find out about me through the internet or personal networks. A large part of my job was going round being introduced to fellow wizards, other leaders and influencers in that space. I could email or pick up the phone to a very wide range of people in that world and stand a good chance of a reply. If you wanted me to speak at a conference, I would provide a half-page CV.

How did I train to become a wizard (not that, at the time, I fully understood what I was doing)? In the Civil Service I had two classic apprenticeship roles, working as a private secretary to two wizards (a cabinet minister and a permanent secretary). Being a headhunter was an intensive training in working with wizards and would-be wizards; I was taught by two masters of the art, Anthony Saxton and Stephen Bampfylde. I became known in the voluntary sector and was selected through a semi-competitive process to join the Diana, Princess of Wales Memorial Fund as a trustee. Becoming treasurer there was a 'battlefield promotion'; we lost a highly experienced treasurer in the middle of fierce litigation when only a fool would have considered joining us. By the end of that you might have called me a half-wizard in the non-profit end of the British establishment.

At that point I was introduced to the Refugee Council, who were looking for a chair. I went through a public, competitive interview process and came second. Someone with substantial chairing experience and a CBE was picked ahead of me but, within a few weeks and before any announcement was made, the individual withdrew. I was asked if I was still interested and answered, 'Yes'.

What did it feel like to be a wizard for six years? That sounds an easy question but is harder than it looks. If you are a wizard with 'L' plates, as I was at the beginning, you're concentrating too hard on doing the right thing to notice much else. If the status becomes habitual, you don't notice for different reasons. But using this book's chapter headings as a prompt for what being muggle crust feels like, I can ask myself what felt different. Here's a taste.

A lot of it felt like being a junior version of the Queen: travelling to different parts of the country, being introduced to lots of people, showing interest in them and their work, accepting hospitality and meals, saying a few words. The muggle in me worried that I wasn't 'doing' anything substantial, but I learned a lot about making an impact in different ways. And before the six years were up there were challenging, hands-on times when it came home to me that, if I had not taken the trouble to spend time (however briefly) with many people around the country, the organisation would have been in trouble. I would have failed in my role.

There were memorable moments behind the scenes. We had put in place an agreed strategy clearly focused on the interests of refugees rather than growing the organisation financially (as the largest charity in our sector we were regularly accused of prioritising the latter). It felt good when the chief executive came to tell me that, in line with our strategy, she did not intend to bid for government funds for repatriation assistance. Our strategy was clear and returning people whose asylum claims had been rejected was no part of it. The satisfaction from being part of a top leadership group was, on a number of occasions, shaping outcomes. Of course, there were also many times when we were on the receiving end of government decisions which we had no power to change.

The Refugee Council had what I called 'a good anti-Mugabe constitution' (there were many refugees from Zimbabwe) so chairs were limited to six years in the role. There was a final AGM, speeches and a presentation. I chose my stepping-down day so that I could spend my last couple of hours visiting the staff winter party in Brixton, without any VIP formalities. Many of the duties of a chair are extrovert but this was my introvert self coming through, wanting to reflect, with the help of a couple of bottles of Becks, on what was ending. I liked the idea of doing this in the midst of music and a younger generation which would continue without me.

As I sat, a young woman came over and introduced herself as a volunteer. She knew that I was the chair stepping down, and asked me what my best day in the role had been. I laughed and said that it was easier to think of challenging days, and then acknowledged that I had dodged her question. After a silence I said, 'I think the best thing has been seeing Jade's smile.' Jade Amoli-Jackson[5] was an exceptionally loyal volunteer and refugee from Uganda, where she had lost several members of her family. This included retrieving from the Ugandan government the body of her husband; she got it back with his head missing. That was not the end of her trials. Jade has a fantastic smile. On the edge of tears the volunteer said, 'That's so moving'. I hadn't intended to move anyone or anything, but maybe my answer hints at the payoff for me of six years as a wizard.

I'm not a wizard now. That's a matter of fact, not humility. We could go through my list of contacts, whittle it down to those who might well return my call or respond to my email if I got in touch to ask for a favour. It's a pot-pourri of wizards, muggle crust, junior muggles and artisans, who run across as varied a galaxy of worlds as luck and effort have let me explore. But there isn't a group at the top of any one activity where they all know (or know of) me, and I know (or know of) them.

Looking back, two moments stand out as personal decisions not to pursue wizardry above other things: when I stepped down from being a headhunter, and a few years later when I stepped down from the Refugee Council. I could have tried to find new supplies of pixie dust. However, there are more things to life than wizardry, and I wanted to discover them.

---

5   You can read Jade Amoli-Jackson's story in her book *Moving A Country* (CreateSpace, 2013).

THE EIGHTH LESSON

GET FEEDBACK

Feedback is the breakfast
of champions

LET'S GET TO THE FLIP right away: feedback may be the breakfast of champion muggles, but it's the porridge and kippers of wizards.

The breakfast of champions idea was carved into the muggle mind by Ken Blanchard, who sold more than 13 million copies of *The One Minute Manager*. In 2015, he wrote in a blog post[6]:

> I first heard the phrase *feedback is the breakfast of champions* from a former colleague, Rick Tate. He explained it in sports terms. Can you imagine training for the Olympics with no one telling you how fast you ran or how high you jumped? That idea seems ludicrous, yet many people operate in a vacuum in organizations, not knowing how well they are doing on any given task.

The impact of Blanchard's carving has been immense. Every year around the world violent swearing is provoked by the need to stuff the mouth of an employer's computer system with 'feedback', which could be more than thirty scale ratings and two paragraphs of free text on each of more than ten colleagues: sufficient breakfast for several airport hotel buffets. Yet few who consume it turn into champions.

That feedback is *not* the breakfast of wizards is easy to demonstrate: try giving a wizard some. It would then be wise to stand back. However, it *is* their porridge and kippers. Five-

6   https://howwelead.org/2015/01/07/feedback-is-the-breakfast-of-champions-2/

star breakfast menus always offer porridge and kippers, along with fresh fruit, bacon rolls and egg-white-only omelettes with herbs from the garden. Every day every wizard is open to feedback, just as they are gratified by the possibility of choosing porridge or kippers, but most days they will choose something else. On the other hand, why shouldn't ambitious muggles sign up to eat porridge and kippers every day?

This simple flip is enough to exhibit the whole muggle-wizard economy in microcosm. To advance in their world, muggles must embrace feedback. A lot of it is stodgy and not very interesting (porridge) while some of it is unpleasant and sticks in the throat (kippers), but the process of digestion does make ambitious muggles more effective. In the muggle crust, believing in feedback is obligatory. Thanks to these feedback mechanisms, large parts of the world run more effectively.

This benefits wizards directly (when they use muggle-managed services) but also frees them up to occupy themselves in different, magical ways. These include spouting all kinds of crap to nearby muggles, which the latter gracefully receive as feedback. What a hoot! There's more. Seeking feedback is a first-class muggle badge. 'I was wondering if you had any feedback for me on how yesterday's break-out sessions went?'

Having flexed his muscles on *The One Minute Manager*, Blanchard went on to launch the book *Lead Like Jesus*. Indeed, the Gospels show us how the feedback flip works. First we need to work out whether Jesus was a muggle, wizard or artisan.

In relation to established Roman and Jewish society, Jesus was an artisan, not even a muggle (let alone muggle crust): a carpenter turned rabble-rouser from the back country who had never dined with anyone who mattered. As a low-life, Jesus was battered with continuous feedback from the Pharisees and Sadducees, which in the end crucified him.

But in relation to the movement he established, Jesus was a wizard. He was the nucleus of the group of disciples who followed him and whose inner circle came to know each other well. They were wizards, and many of their names survive in the Gospels. (The Gospels also suggest that Jesus opted for the Cinderella approach to recruiting new wizards, roaming around to accost unknown fishermen and others. Maybe Judas worked for McKinsey.)

What's clear from the Gospels is that, as a wizard, any feedback which Jesus received from his growing band of disciples was occasional at best. At his baptism Jesus is told that his heavenly father is pleased, and at his first miracle the steward at the wedding feast pronounces the new wine to be excellent. But as his followers gather and his wizard status acquires solidity, good intentions about feedback seem to peter out. There is no sign that 'happy sheets' were distributed after the Sermon on the Mount, nor do any of the parables end with a disciple remonstrating, 'I think that's a bit long? And too harsh on the Pharisees'.

THE NINTH LESSON

DON'T FAIL

Cultivate anxiety

GOVERNANCE: THE ACT OR MANNER of governing; the office or function of governing. See also: wizardry.

Western Australia, November 2018. At four in the morning the driver gets down from his cab to check an issue with a cargo of rock the colour of rust and dried blood. 20,000 tonnes of iron ore are being pulled in 260 wagons by four locomotives, so the check takes some time – during which the driverless train takes off, reaching nearly 70 mph before being forcibly derailed an hour later. Shit happens, but no one is hurt.

'Shit happens' is not the attitude which gets you promoted into the muggle crust. The crust motto is 'cultivate anxiety'. Its sworn enemy is Murphy's Law (anything which can go wrong, will). Most muggles who want to get things done turn stones daily to spot unnoticed details. Their imaginations torment them with lurid accounts of what will follow shit happening on their watch. To get into the muggle crust and stay there, don't let mistakes happen – don't fail.

As by now we expect, this muggle mindset pays off for wizards in lots of ways. Wizards share in the general benefits of a reduced-shit world, with practically no chance of getting personally speckled with brown stuff – as the ferocity of their anger demonstrates when their invisible protection fails. Witness Prime Minister Theresa May's party conference speech in October, 2017. The nation had a glorious future, she explained on television, while letters fell off the set behind her. She was not pleased.

The muggle crust struggles hard not to fail because failure is a terrible thing; wizards don't fail because they can't. Wizards learn the opposite of cultivating anxiety. The job of wizards is to do *great things*. This entitles them to breathe air from which the possibility of failure has been scrubbed. Ultimately, the world will not let them down. To be a wizard is to find this obvious, and to live out that conviction. Convictions of other kinds – for example, in prison – are no block to reclaiming a lofty perch in society: after all an imprisoned wizard still knows (and is known by) the people who matter.

It is painful to watch the extraordinary number of political wizards – Dominic Cummings for example – who have grasped what a wonderful teaching moment coronavirus has provided on this lesson. But the greater our muggle anger at these offences, the more we risk blaming things on individual villains instead of noticing a structural feature of the wizard world. So let's take an example from 2007, with a very unpromising grey 'villain', steeped in the muggle virtues.

In Britain, the Comptroller and Auditor General (C&AG) is a unique role with special powers and protections, tasked by law with chasing down wasteful spending. The C&AG is expected to be a paragon of economy, virtue and doing things properly. The job has a good claim to be Britain's Chief Muggle Officer. In 2007 the holder of the office, Sir John Bourn – no Cummings he, a civil servant through and through – was exposed as having claimed for 43 overseas trips, travelling first class (frequently with his wife). On exposure the tax authorities demanded from Bourn fines and back taxes on his inflated 'expenses'. The following year *Private Eye* reported that Bourn had successfully passed the £100,000 tax penalty bill on to…the taxpayer.

Bourn's interview with *The Telegraph* on his departure is a masterclass in wizard thinking. Had he failed? Was he leaving under a cloud? Far from it.

> Not as far as I'm concerned… I do not think I've been [in the job] too long. I've been successful for the whole twenty years.

The 'we' in the next quotation shows the elite nature of the group of which Bourn knows he is – and will remain – a member.

> We are all potential victims of disaffected employees or ex-employees… This is the world we live in: if you can't stand the heat, get out of the kitchen.

As the world plunges into a global financial crisis, Bourn, then seventy-four, explains that he's stepping down because the law obliges him to start drawing his pension. But life won't be dull: who better to chair the body that monitors the quality of public company auditing? More than a decade later the wizard was still going strong: he was listed as senior adviser to a charity dedicated to 'thought leadership and best practice in governance', the Foundation for Governance Research and Education.

The effrontery is breath-taking. But are wizards purely parasitical in the muggle-wizard economy?

If all planet Earth offered was muggles and muggle crust, we would be looking at a prairie landscape with fields of cultivated anxiety as far as the eye could see. It would be a society trapped by fear of the unknown. If instead Earth was home only to wizards, our view would be of a sky full of brilliant stars which never fall to the ground. But at the horizon where wizardry and the muggle crust meet, some genuinely new possibilities can break through.

The horizon is a long way away. To journey there requires hope. You can't brew hope out of anxiety. Maybe wizards do something useful.

THE TENTH LESSON

THE ROUTE TO
THE TOP IS OPEN

It's all about talent and hard work

In each person's petrol tank is their own blend of hard work and ability. Frankly, some people don't have a lot. But get motoring! The route to the top is open. As the motivational slogan has it, it's your attitude (or your aptitude) which determines your altitude.

Behold the steel frame which holds up every part of the muggle world. It inspires us to get up and work hard. It gives us a reason to respect our boss. It reassures when doubts attack: when you wonder whether you have achieved anything, look down and see how far talent and effort have brought you. Of course, nothing's perfect, but if a sufficient degree of meritocracy did not undergird the muggle world, we would not be surrounded by skyscrapers of human achievement – in industry, science, sports, education and the arts. Be in awe: talent and tenacity built these things.

We previously introduced the idea of glass ceilings. When we look up, merit seems to apply all the way. We see no block. So – by and large, nothing's perfect – the people with offices on the top floor must be exceptionally talented or hardworking, or both. Good for them.

Looking down from that floor, the elite also sees no block. This reassures them about their own success. Luck may have mopped their brow but, by God, they showed what it takes to triumph over intense competition. The route to the top is open. Wizards gracefully acknowledge that not everyone can match them in talent and tenacity. Ping Fu, the tiger lady co-founder of a software company, puts it like this: 'If you don't believe in the glass ceiling, it does not exist.'[7]

Do they exist? We can deal with this briefly because, in a way, a large part of this book is a test of them. The first kind of evidence is numerical, which is how the glass ceiling idea started. Up to a certain point in the sky we see lots of swallows and other birds flying, and above that point only other birds. That is evidence that something is going on, but it isn't conclusive. Perhaps swallows weren't built to fly that high, or they choose not to – these arguments may be thin but people make them. The other kind of evidence is experiential: you smack into it and it hurts. Only the muggle crust are likely to have this experience, which is why they are the focus of this book.

The more you take Ping Fu's advice and *don't* believe in glass ceilings, the more powerful the difference between muggles and wizards becomes. By not believing in them you solemnly declare that there are no unearned goodies: what you have, you have earned, and what you may deserve in the future, you will get. The road is open. This belief is a force of astronomical scale: in a meritocracy, it is the sun which rises every morning without fail.

If you make it to the glass ceiling and knock for admission, hope that the knock isn't answered by a newbie wizard. If the wizard is still wearing her 'L' plates, she knows that many wizard eyes are on her. She must demonstrate her understanding that admission through apprenticeship is rare and only for senior wizards to offer. If she leaves the gate to the top open, she will be back in the muggle crust in a flash.

---

7   Interviewed for *Quartz* in 2013.

I'm mixed-race (Chinese and English). Along with my brother and sister, I come from splicing the genes of an only child from an English country vicarage together with some from a cosmopolitan family of six children in Shanghai. Both my parents were highly educated although, as my Shanghainese mother explained to me, my father's Cambridge education did not include discovering how to boil an egg.

My mother was equally fired up about the practice of teaching and theories of how people develop; she became a school principal, founded a new secondary school in a working-class estate and did a doctorate in Chinese learners' difficulties in mastering English. So it's not surprising that one day I found at home an academic article on challenges in the development of mixed-race children. (I'm guessing that I was about ten. I probably wasn't supposed to be in her bedroom.) Through childhood and into university difficulties in belonging were prominent for me, mixed-race being part of it. In fact, I was a bit disappointed when British ethnic monitoring forms improved and I could no longer tick 'None of the above' as my identity. But as an adult what I've learned about discriminatory barriers has mainly come through opportunities to understand selection processes and the lives of others. I gave one example on page 82.

A less dramatic but not less vivid example came early in my time as a headhunter. I remember being delighted that a black man in his thirties had made it onto a shortlist. Nothing the selection committee had said or done made me doubt that its members had a strong commitment to equal opportunities. Ahead of his interview, the man pressed me on whether his candidacy was token: how seriously should he take it? Putting myself in his shoes, I couldn't say it was irrational for him to wonder this – which meant that there was an objective obstacle right there. No white man on the shortlist wasted time and energy wondering such a thing.

Later I worked on some searches for non-executive directors where my clients were senior figures from the FTSE 100 world – men and women. The results were mixed. In one case I concluded that the task the chair had engaged us to do was to discover relevantly skilled individuals whom he had met at dinner but forgotten. (If they were women or from ethnic minorities, so much the better.) If we produced candidates whom he had met at dinner and still remembered, then we lacked creativity and were a waste of money. When we produced people whom he hadn't met at dinner, then they plainly weren't any good, and neither were we for failing to spot that deficiency for ourselves.

At the time I understood a lot less about muggles and wizards. Now I would say that just as rationality becomes personal (the second lesson), so does merit. People who have been wizards for a long time come to think that if they don't know an individual, she cannot be any good: that is what their world is like to live in.

The problems of meritocracy were prophetically analysed by the sociologist Michael Young in 1958[8]. The more society modernises and becomes merit-based up to the muggle crust, the more the sunlight passing benignly through the glass ceiling nurtures the belief that meritocracy is increasing all the way up – because the rules are the same, aren't they? There's no visible boundary.

The consequence is that muggles and wizards both overestimate how much talent wizards have. Muggles feel inferior in a way which isn't justified, while wizards know that they really are superior beings who got to the top on merit. This isn't simply about feelings: misunderstanding elites increases their power.

The way I defined elites on page 13 foreshadows one of this book's claims: that every meritocracy produces its own glass ceiling. Build something as tall as you like using the steel girders of talent and tenacity: the occupants of the penthouses will still become wizards. The route to the top may be open, but it is never straightforward.

---

8   *The Rise of the Meritocracy*, Transaction Publishers.

Three action takeaways

AT THIS POINT, we have covered the ten fundamental climbing lessons and are hovering around somewhere near that glass ceiling. In Part Three we will ponder on a few more essential insights as we begin to find ourselves, on occasion, breathing the same rarefied air as the wizards, stepping up into that heady space from time to time.

But first let us ask: *so what?* So what if there are muggles and wizards? How does unpacking this help anyone? Well, addressing it through these next three takeaways from The Senior Executive's Survival Guide will help ensure your survival when dealing with wizards, as well as assist you in becoming one, if you want to do that. We must also consider how we might go about changing this system. These three takeaways offer packages of advice rather than single mantras or rules; which takeaway speaks to you will depend on what you want.

THE FIRST
ACTION TAKEAWAY

HOW TO SURVIVE
ELITES

TO FIND SOME OF THE most admirable leaders our society
has to offer, go to the muggle crust. Sure, some have turned
cynical. Others are worn out. Prolonged exposure to wizards
can do this.

But in my experience, that leaves within the muggle crust
a richer seam of hidden heroes and heroines than any other
slice of society I know (wizards definitely included). Together,
the muggle crust make hospitals, ambulance services, power
stations and the internet deliver. They have responsibilities
which can get them sacked: a screw-up on their patch puts
them more at risk than any wizard. They challenge stupid
promises behind closed doors, at least until the tide of idiocy
proves unstoppable. When those stupidities are still promised,
they face up to the horrible leadership and management
challenges of trying to make the best of them.

The bigger their achievements, the less likely they are to be
recognised (even by their peers). Why? Because they are loyal.
Short of a whistle-blowing situation, it goes deep against the
muggle grain, as well as the legal contracts which pay their
mortgages, to wash their organisation's dirty linen in public.
Even in an organisation with a large muggle crust, many
things make individual members who are under pressure
quite isolated. Sharing with peer executives crap which they
don't need to know in order to get some recognition of your
own achievement sounds like any or all of the following:
boasting, gossip, politicking, damaging morale or weakness.
Of course, any boastable success will be trumpeted, but with
wizards' names in headline position.

There are reasons to worry about this, despite very many people being worse paid and worse placed than the muggle crust – for example, the migrant construction workers in Mumbai whom we met on page 33. First, human lives and families go by the board. The ten lessons demonstrate that senior executive burn-out is a design feature, not a bug. The muggle crust live by those lessons 24/7. They believe they must exemplify those lessons to others. They are up against a glass ceiling which they can feel but not see; and they are dispensable. Simply put, they may not survive.

However much danger money the muggle crust get, their burn-out is bad news for the rest of us. When the muggle crust is constantly tired, threatened or burned out, stupid ideas win more of the behind-closed-doors arguments. An elite of wizards running amok is as bad as it gets. Shockingly, a large swathe of British public service appears to have reached this point. This costs lives.

Next, if the best of the muggle crust don't survive, or survive but think 'sod wizardry for a career', lesser people become wizards. The bias in our top leadership pool towards ignorance and arrogance increases.

And if the muggle crust contains some of our most inspiring heroes and heroines, the rest of us need to know some of their stories, alongside the stories of brilliant artisans and ethical wizards. Well-founded hope is in short supply. We need in the public domain not just whistle-blowers' secrets but senior executives' inspiring courage. We need to know that above the frontline keyworkers whom we sometimes applaud isn't simply an ethical and professional void.

If visitors from outer space arrive one day and ask to be

taken to 'our leaders', we'll take them to the wizards. But if instead they ask to meet our best leaders, our best managers, our best thinkers and problem-solvers, our most ethical role models, we should head for the muggle crust. You may be in the muggle crust precisely because you are the best at what you care about. The wizardry does (thank God) contain some spectacular, admirable talents, but the high achiever in the muggle crust is likely to be as good, or better, than many wizards at what the organisation most deeply values. At the muggle-wizard boundary, the game changes. Wizards play by different rules, including all the time having to monitor their connectedness to other wizards. The best place for earning a gold medal for being excellent at what you have most cared about is probably the muggle crust. You may already have succeeded more than you realised. Take a bow.

What I most often hear next from members of the muggle crust whom I've had the privilege to coach is laughter: 'So *that* is why things are so weird around here, and why thinking smarter, working harder and delivering results doesn't automatically lift me higher.' On the heels of laughter comes an enlivening sense of choice: 'I don't have to try to become a wizard, do I? So should I like or respect them?' I will say more about that in the next chapter.

Simply grasping that the wizard game is different already gives the muggle crust more power. For their own survival wizards are good at spotting when this penny has dropped. One day a member of the muggle crust is sitting down with their wizard boss. Suddenly, somehow, the muggle's body language sends a message, and the wizard realises: *this one knows*. The colour of Superman's underwear is no longer secret. And what can flow from that to the benefit of us all is the muggle crust having greater confidence in pointing out those parts of wizard visions which are sheer nonsense.

This awareness should be a win-win game. A wizard boss and an aware executive can accomplish a lot based on mutual respect. Now the executive can see why his boss spends so much time managing what other wizards know and think about what the first wizard is doing. It may not be an over-delicate ego. Knowing, and knowing of, each other is at the heart of wizard magic. This is what breathing is like at the top of the mountain: it's different. If the respect is mutual, an aware wizard boss and an aware muggle executive can launch bold initiatives with great confidence – bolder and more thought-through than either could on their own.

However, knowledge is still power even if the wizard prefers to believe in her own infallibility. Look again at the first ten lessons on the Contents page. If these were the bars in your mental prison, let them fall. You might want to change some of your habits. But even if you don't, know that when you are in a tough spot, moves are available to you which you may not have spotted before.

Keep in mind that what you have so painfully learned as a muggle is not wasted. Your hard-won capabilities remain valuable. Without them you would not be this close to the top. Without them, you would not be able to be successful as a wizard, should you succeed in becoming one (for example, see Lesson Six on taking responsibility). Remember the cleaner, the twenty-five-year-old and the director in the lift: in a sense, the only thing that will gradually change is what you notice and what strikes you as obvious.

A practical first exercise is to ask, is your boss a wizard? If she has prepared an up-to-date CV and you know how long it is, that may be a clue. But since the stakes are high, don't rely on this short-cut. Instead think about who at the top would return your boss's message or call if she had a personal request? And does your boss see the world in a way which has enough in common with the 'powers that be' for her to be 'one of us'?

THE SECOND
ACTION TAKEAWAY

HOW TO JOIN
ELITES

THE PREVIOUS CHAPTER WAS for the many hidden heroes in the muggle crust, and I'm unembarrassed to wear my heart on my sleeve for them. But on its own it could make wizards sound at best like a waste of space and at worst like villains. So before describing how to join an elite, let us give that ambition some dignity. Some wizards (like some muggle crust) are bad guys or ladies, but there's nothing about being a wizard which means *you* have to be.

I'm proud to have been given the privilege, and experience, of being a wizard in a world which matters to me. The more time I spent with wizards, the greater the joy in getting to hang out with a handful of profoundly impressive individuals: moral and professional giants. There were others, of course, like Henry in 'The room where it happens'. The wizardry in business does have more than its fair share of shits[9]; fortunately, they are not the whole story.

I am not against wizards; I am against a widespread misunderstanding of their world which narrows the pool from which wizards are drawn, and which gives those who do make it a level of power and adulation which impoverishes the rest of us. What does that mean for you? If you have spent much of your life thinking that wizardry is not for you (because that world doesn't want you or because you think you wouldn't want that world), then the agenda of this book is to disturb that assumption. And if like me you spent much of your life thinking that 'up' is the obvious place to go, that

9   For the reason which I explored in my first novel, *MBA* (Lightning Books, 2015).

becoming a wizard would be a deserved success and not becoming one might be failure, then the agenda of this book is to disturb that assumption as well.

I'm writing this in one of my favourite places, beside Lake Garda. If the wind manages to meet my pernickety requirements – not too fast, not too slow – I'll be on a windsurfer this afternoon, trying to tack (do an upwind turn) faster. My current tacking is serviceable but ungainly; I want to be able to handle faster winds and a choppier lake surface. On the water I'm trying to persuade my feet to take a leap of faith: to move in fewer steps to where they need to be, trusting that in the meantime a combination of the sail and the rest of me will have moved the board to where it needs to be when the feet land.

My feet have excellent reasons not to have faith, because the rest of me has yet to learn its part in the movement reliably. So I try, try and try again, a lot of the time ending up in the water. The thing is, trying with a cynic's mind is doomed: I'm more or less guaranteed to fail, and the cynic delightedly shrieks, 'See? I told you so'. What struck me while out on the water yesterday was that to throw off the inner cynic, I almost need an irrational belief that I can't fail – one which will somehow regenerate itself to fuel another attempt if I do fail. I need an inner wizard. And I haven't taken leave of my senses, because there's a long list of things which I can do easily now (they have become obvious) which for a long time were a miserably slow struggle.

Wizards have a social and belief structure which supports the belief that they cannot fail (the ninth lesson). That belief is dangerously corrupting but has social uses. A muggle-wizard economy can make more, and more imaginative, leaps of progress than one in which everyone is limited by the lessons of muggledom.

Wizards' social and belief structure also helps them cope with living on the cutting edge of meritocracy. A meritocracy works best when what is good or merit-worthy is calculable by fair, objective principles. Any such calculations can be managed by the muggle crust. What's thrown upstairs to the wizards are harder problems in which what should count as good isn't obvious any more. Wizard work has to be done without that grounding, so wizards need to be anchored through relationships, shared beliefs and other ways. Knowing (and knowing of) each other can spiral down into 'group think', but a social matrix can also spiral up into a powerful problem-solving tool. At its best, and in healthy relationship with a muggle crust, a wizard world isn't an elite self-indulgence, but a rich, creative resource. There can be useful stuff along with the shit.

Why not try becoming a wizard? You might like it or you might not. You might succeed or fail. But there's no knowing without trying. If you want to try, the analysis of the muggle-wizard economy offered in this book leads to six tips.

Tip One: there's no short cut.

Now and again individuals such as Donald Trump vault into the wizardry without bothering to master the first ten lessons. Usually they fall out of the sky as fast as they shoot up. The rest of us have to master the lessons. Even princelings (*see page 15*) have to learn muggle stuff if they want to become full wizards.

Tip Two: study how the ten lessons change for wizards.

To be a wizard needs two things. First, the world needs to show up for you in a similar way to how it does for wizards. Wizards are colourful, so individuality is fine, but much of what is obvious to them needs to be obvious to you. Most of Part Two has concentrated on this. Second, you need pixie dust to know (or know of) as many wizards as possible, and be known (or known of) by them. Tips Four, Five and Six speak to this, with Tip Three as a vital precaution.

Tip Three: check carefully where you are in relation to the muggle crust.

You are in the muggle crust if above you there are plenty of wizards. Apply the test described for your boss on page 122. If you are not yet in the muggle crust, take care. Applying Tips Four, Five or Six will backfire. Muggles above you will have at least three reasons to block your career: you are not doing the right muggle stuff; you are annoyingly uppity; and you may be a threat.

Tip Four: when you meet wizards, show your potential.
Show that you grasp some fundamentals of wizard thinking
but want help to get it right. Some psychologists describe
four stages in learning a skill, such as how to drive a car. The
starting point is unconscious incompetence (I don't know
stuff, and don't realise that I don't know). The next step is
conscious incompetence (I still don't know stuff, but now
I realise that there is stuff I don't know). The third step is
conscious competence (I can do stuff, but only slowly and with
a lot of thought). The final step is unconscious competence (I
do stuff instinctively; it's become obvious).

To start with, you want to come over to wizards as moving
from the second step into the third: you understand that there
is a lot about wizardry which you don't know, but slowly
you are getting some of it under your belt. Even if you have
sussed out more than this, keep it to yourself: wizards don't
like smart-arses any more than anyone else does.

Tip Five: find wizard sponsors.
The first-best, second-best and third-best wizard school is
apprenticeship. Wizardry involves lots of things that are best
learned by getting close to individuals who are willing to
share, including discussing their own mistakes. Try to find
one of these as a *teaching mentor.*

How might you set about that? Do you know a wizard
who is highly experienced and generous? Don't be shy about
approaching them. It doesn't matter that you can't think why
they would be interested in you. If you ask in a way which
genuinely values their expertise and doesn't box them into a
corner, the answer might be 'no' but they will feel flattered,

positive about you and more likely to notice you in the future.

To ask in a good way, start by saying why you think they would be a terrific mentor – be honest and objective, rather than crawling. Next, spell out the obvious consequence: most likely they are already fully occupied with mentees. Finally, give them several constructive ways of responding to your ask. Since they know many more senior people than you (the definition of a wizard!), can they think of one you might approach instead? Were any books or other teaching materials powerful for them?

A different kind of sponsor is an *introducer*: a wizard who will introduce you to other wizards and invite you to things. Sometimes the same wizard has the time and ability both to teach and to introduce, but be open to the possibility of splitting the roles.

Finally, the wizards you need may not be in your organisation. How far does the elite stretch to which the wizards above you belong? Who could call the wizards above you with a personal request and get their call returned? Your teaching mentor could be a retired wizard, while your introducer might be a journalist, a supplier, a headhunter or something else.

Tip Six: in the end, you have to cross the river of being personally known.
I can only describe this from personal experience. The river feels horrendously wide: you do not know many, or any, wizards ('know' in the sense that they would return your phone call if you wanted to ask a favour) and they certainly do not know you. In the distance the far bank looks impossibly

crowded: you imagine that there are tens, maybe hundreds, of wizards who know everybody, and everybody knows them (or so it seems to you). Between your status and theirs there are many rapids and fast currents which could sweep you away. You dream of a helicopter (being dropped into a job which gives you an admission ticket to lots of important relationships)!

Throw this mindset away right now. A lot of people give off that they are better connected than they are. Some people who 'know' lots of people are odious; no one returns their calls if they can help it. And very few wizards got helicopter rides. They stood where you stand, and found their way across. They had to get their feet wet exactly as you do now.

Crossing the river means discovering that, although you can't see them until you get close, there are places where flat stones lie under just a couple of inches of water and can carry your weight. Look for the first stone, one close to you, not the whole sequence; even from the other side you will never be able to see the whole sequence.

Finding each stone is *one small, bullshit-free step* towards demonstrating that you have a modest, but steadily increasing, stock of useful *knowledge about wizards* of the kind which other wizards have. For example, your first step might be to buy a ticket to a conference to hear a famous wizard speak. You read up about them, listen as they answer questions, and ask a question yourself (you absolutely don't go up to them and start acting as their friend – no bullshit, remember).

Your next step might be to chat to a muggle at your level who has worked in that wizard's organisation (much easier with social media). Pick up some impressions, however distant. Then an opportunity suddenly comes up: you are in a wizard meeting and the famous wizard's name comes up, or you bring it into the conversation because it is relevant. (Of course, this won't work if you introduce the name of someone who to you is a big shot, but to the wizards is just muggle crust. But you know how to work out who is a wizard: assemble your information patiently.)

You venture an informed question (for example, 'I know Steve's famous for being a hard bastard, but is that actually right? I heard something which made me wonder'). Don't claim knowledge that you don't have. But show that you realise that knowing stuff about wizards is an important game, and while you are only a beginner, you have shown up at the game ready to play. With a bit of luck, you'll witness a short burst of conversation in which wizards do what they do all the time, which is check out with each other their knowledge of each other.

And now you have some wizard-quality knowledge about Steve: a first flat stone under the surface of the river. Here are three examples of ways you could use that knowledge, to find the next stepping stone, one of which is a total fail:

• the next time you go to a conference which Steve is addressing, you can say how keen you are to meet him because you know how highly his peers think of him (and if challenged you can back that up);

• in a conversation with a different wizard, you can gain leverage by implying that you know Steve and giving an informed opinion about him;

• or you could trade insights with someone you trust who sells to people like Steve, getting an insight in return about another wizard, or perhaps an invitation to a drinks party.

Yes, the second one is a total fail – it's bullshit.

Finally, a word about golf – is that (or a different diversion) the key to getting to know, and be known by, your local wizards, supposing that a group of them do that stuff?

I don't want to rule it out. At one end of the spectrum is the scenario in which several high-powered wizards belong to and regularly play at an exclusive golf club to which you, potentially, have access. First off, this sounds suspiciously like a cross between the set-up to a John Grisham plot and the Trump presidency. Second, one of my clients was confronted on a regular basis with whether to go and spend the weekend getting 'bladdered' on a Portuguese golf course with the CEO and his cronies, or to spend time with his child. He chose his child – and still made it into the wizardry. Excluding the Trump presidency, I have never come across wizards encountering a muggle on a golf course and deciding to bring him or her into their inner council.

At the other end of my imaginary spectrum is discovering that a wizard is keen on five-a-side football or wants to learn coding, which happen to be strong suits for you. Or organising something fun as part of a company awayday which makes the wizard your new best friend. Or discovering and sharing a wizard's enthusiasm on social media. Or showing enough interest in people that the wizard cares about to help one of them get a great opportunity. If these things are possibilities for you, there's no reason to dismiss them.

But in the context of crossing our wide river, my picture of all of these things is a rickety wooden jetty which sticks out from some land to which you have private access. It could be a head start across the river which others don't have, but beware traps and rotten planks. Even with that head start, you have a long way to go, learning to do the slow stuff which I described earlier. There are a lot of wizards to get to know, and they probably don't all belong to the same golf club.

A final caution: core to the definition of wizard is not just the pixie dust but a substantially shared mindset. In a meritocratic wizardry a fundamental of that mindset will be being bloody good at the day job. Think about the balance in where you put your energy.

THE THIRD
ACTION TAKEAWAY

HOW TO CHANGE
ELITES
(Part One)

THERE ARE TWO POWERFUL, clashing reasons to put two fingers up to old hierarchies and careers built around them.

Some young people will be lucky enough to have the confidence and a secure home base (even if the security is in the mind rather than the property market) to be freer than any earlier generation from having to live out a career climbing someone else's ladders. Creativity is key: everything else will soon be done by robots. Sometimes the kaleidoscope of choice may be a headache, but it's still a blinding opportunity. Let's remake the world. Who needs elites?

Others in the same generation may feel they have been handed a particularly shocking collection of short straws: unfairly limited access to opportunities, in the middle of a dramatic economic collapse on a rapidly degenerating planet, with very little organisational and institutional legacy capable of rising to the challenges of the future. We have to remake the world. Who needs elites?

If you think that something is broken in Western society then I am with you – and I hope you will be with me in Part Three. At this point we face a quandary. Our situation is so urgent that a new world cannot come too soon. However, we are the chief threat to ourselves (and the planet). If haste leads us to miss what's really broken, we may simply make things worse.

Management wizards Gary Hamel and Michele Zanini think what's broken is how we wire up people to form organisations. Their book *Humanocracy*[10] is a call to arms for better, bolder wiring: creating new kinds of workplaces in which every participant is accountable to colleagues rather than a boss; no one has to waste time sucking up or playing political games; and influence and reward are dependent upon abilities, not rank. They ask, why not a world in which: 'You [are] never given reason to feel inferior to the higher-ups?' (*p. ix*)

Whether Hamel and Zanini's world is possible turns on why the pattern described in Part Two of this book exists. That's why discussing radical societal change must wait for Part Three. However, if your experience is at all like mine, the courageous change advocate and the individual anxiously trying to survive in the middle of chaos are often the same person. If this is you, let me live up to the promise of this part – a survival guide – and deliver the best advice I can for staying afloat. Is this me addressing my twenty-year-old self? Absolutely.

If one person's survival seems a small thing compared to saving humanity, it isn't. Hamel and Zanini's sub-title is, 'Creating Organizations as Amazing as the People Inside Them'. Writing Part Three turned upside down my understanding of the relationship between the ordinariness of 'amazing' people (elites) and the amazingness of ordinary people. Don't just stay with me for this journey: I would like to help you survive, thrive and change the world afterwards! So:

First, very carefully tend deep relationships (plural) which

10   *Humanocracy: Creating Organizations as Amazing as the People Inside Them*, Harvard Business Review Press (2020).

nurture and energise you. The more chaotic our future, the more careers start going all over the place, the more important will be core relationships with quality, honesty and concern for each other if you are to hold on to your identity. *Without them you may find in time that you do not know who you are.* If you grasp this point better than many of your friends, you might end up doing the lion's share of the work which keeps those relationships going. That's particularly so when children are involved, or moves to faraway places come about. You can't and shouldn't do all the work a relationship needs, but don't become too sensitive about equality.

Second, if you can, keep one or two relationships with the ambitious. (Some of the ambitious will drop you if you are not 'upwardly mobile' like they are. But not all the ambitious are shits.) Why? Because there's a downside to exploring an infinite Milky Way of new career possibilities. Despite those possibilities, Earth will remain a stressed, low-attention-span planet. Many future business contacts, let alone employers, will not have the time to decode your career journey and the unique treasures which it offers them. At some point you might need a helping hand from someone in the muggle crust or wizardry of an organisation, in order to get someone to take the time to consider your product or service or to hire you.

Third, don't overlook the possibilities for creating novel paths within apparently conventional structures. Everything was being reinvented even before the 2020 pandemic. Changes impossible to anticipate are coming, as resources such as artificial intelligence are unleashed in the workplace. For example, someone who starts training now as an auditor –

on the face of it not a particularly sexy 'future' job – will have in ten years' time responsibilities, skills and insight which bear no relation to how that work has been done up to now.

An untapped resource for social change is that in the muggle crust are some of our society's best leaders: they face big pressures and pitfalls in their day jobs; when they get a chance to breathe they wonder if they can go further (and whether they want to); and many of them long for a better world as much as you.

Let's investigate what we might use some of that potential to achieve.

PART THREE

BIG QUESTIONS

(What really makes us want
to get to the top)

And breathe...

AT HIGH ALTITUDE breathing may be more difficult than usual and the view may disconcert. Getting to the top left my head buzzing with questions and challenges. Pursuing those questions is where we are going in Part Three. Some of the questions are societal and intellectual. Above all, why? If what I have described at the top of corporate and professional worlds is even partly true, why does this pattern exist? If it does exist, why is it news – why isn't it common sense? After all, we are talking about something big.

But the 'why?' which most shapes Part Three is personal. When I was young I climbed without thinking too much about it. I climbed what was put in front of me, and which turned out to be within reach: going to an elite university, getting a first-class honours degree or getting promoted in the Civil Service 'fast' stream. I was quite a 'thinky' person, fascinated by 'big' questions – for example, philosophical ones or the risk of nuclear annihilation or the return of fascism – but the direction of my own life seemed a much smaller question, fenced in by things which seemed obvious.

That obviousness started unravelling before I was thirty: there was nothing obvious about leaving the Treasury to become a headhunter. That unravelling continued. In Part Three it accelerates as I try as hard as I can to chase down the questions *what kind of success do I really want? And why do I want it?* The answers which came my way shook me.

Might the direction of your own life be, in fact, a very big question? If that interests you I would welcome your company in Part Three.

Exploring society

WHETHER WE CAN change or escape the muggle-wizard economy depends on what kind of thing it is. Is it a coincidental pattern, or something more? Let's begin with a detective story. This story features two guides and some time travel. We're going back to the 1950s. Our 'Dr Who' is Norbert Elias, the German Jewish sociologist whom I mentioned on page 29. Elias fled to Britain in 1935. Steven Pinker's best-seller *The Better Angels of Our Nature* describes him as 'the most important thinker that you have never heard of' – which, in passing, is exactly how wizards introduce members of the muggle crust whom they rate. The Doctor's assistant, John Scotson, is a schoolteacher who became intrigued by social division within a local community in the English Midlands, which the two researchers disguised under the name 'Winston Parva'.

Winston Parva is a town of nearly 5,000 people, mostly

white and working-class. Scotson conducts interviews with members of every thirtieth household on Winston Parva's electoral roll; he also organises a youth club and is able to examine school records. As a result our two detectives know what all the parents of the town's schoolchildren do for a living, and where they live.

Painstakingly they document how, at the end of the 1950s, a social divide springs up within the town – a 'them and us' which sustains itself into new generations without any obvious trigger or support. The detectives can find no racial, religious, educational, employment or financial basis for the division; there is no prior ill will or grievance. But it becomes a clear split: although Winston Parva has only existed since the 1880s, the town's longer-established families stigmatise the new arrivals as inferior. The last influx was more than 100 wartime evacuees.

Elias and Scotson's detective story[11] is a hunt for an invisible badge and some X-ray spectacles. What invisible badge do newcomers carry, a 'newness' which lasts years after their arrival and which they pass on to their children? And what X-ray spectacles do established families automatically grow up with, so that (without being told) their children know which schoolmates not to invite home?

The wartime evacuees arrive with nothing, and are met with generosity. But lurking under the generosity is something else. Stigmatisation ('they are not like us') begins early.

People in the older part of Winston Parva recalled, in interviews, the distress in which the evacuees had arrived.

11   Norbert Elias and John Scotson, *The Established and the Outsiders* (Sage Publications, second edition 1994).

They had lost their homes and most of their family belongings in the bombing. An appeal by a local manufacturer brought an immediate response in the form of clothing, cooking equipment and furniture. Older residents, however, in telling of these events rarely failed to mention that some of the gifts which the newcomers had been given appeared in the pawn shop windows within a few days.[12]

The stigmatisation grows like a weed. Nearly twenty years later, Winston Parva's established families 'know' that the 'new' families (who arrived two decades previously) have children who are more delinquent than their own. It's knowledge which exists independent of any facts: it's just obvious.

The explanation which Elias and Scotson arrive at is disturbingly simple. It's enough that one group has relationships and a common history which the other group does not share. The established families know each other, or of each other, and know about things which happened in the past, including feuds and quarrels (connection doesn't have to mean liking). The newcomers know nothing of these families, Winston Parva's soap-opera history or each other. Being unknown and having no common roots is the badge. The arrivals are strangers, in the way I introduced the word on page 89.

To picture what happens in Winston Parva, imagine two fistfuls of Scrabble tiles taken from the same set. The first are shaken together in a bag while the others lie loose. Later, the loose tiles are added. Weeks later, after many shakings, the first-gathered tiles 'remember' which they were and

---

12   *Op. cit.*, p. 15.

stigmatise the outsiders accordingly.

And the phenomenon passes on to the next generation. Without needing to be told, successive generations of this established human group know that the knowledge they have of each other (and of their shared history) is something precious, to be shared sparingly. Moreover, the stigma creates a connection of sorts between the newcomers, a bond of oppression. From either side of the glass divide – there plainly is a divide because it hurts to walk into it, although no one sees what it is – there is now an 'us' and a 'them'. To keep the whole pattern in place, those in either group who socialise across the divide are punished with lower social status – a finding replicated in much social research.

I first read this detective story in 2008 as part of my doctorate at the University of Hertfordshire. How could I forget it? Personally and professionally, as a headhunter and a coach, I have spent much of my life being drawn to cross over social boundaries. I didn't just read Elias and Scotson's findings: I discovered that I had lived them. The focus of this book and of my first novel[13] is the boundary between muggles and the elite, but boundary-crossing between artisans and muggles is close to my heart and the focus of my second novel[14]. This book is the product of noticing slowly that the behaviour of wizards isn't nearly as special as they might like us to think. It may be rooted in our shared ordinariness.

Writing in *The Guardian* in November 2018, the economist and campaigner, Faiza Shaheen, describes exquisitely the experience of a muggle–wizard interaction:

---

13   *MBA* (Lightning Books, 2015)
14   *Time of Lies* (Lightning Books, 2017)

The first time I went on *The Andrew Marr Show* I was struck by the 'in-crowd' cosiness of it all. In the green room the guests' conversation consisted of showing off about who'd most recently had dinner with David Davis. On another occasion, a Tory grandee completely ignored me. He said hello and goodbye to everyone else (all older, middle class and white) on the panel and just looked past me as if I were invisible. This was particularly weird given that I directly addressed him while we were on air.

For English lower-class behaviour in a small town in the 1950s to provide a key to understanding national elite behaviour seventy years later is a remarkable thing. Could it be that, despite all the differences, the activity unfolding in both settings – what the people involved are trying to accomplish – is connected, or even the same? If so, Winston Parva is a bit like a sociological Los Alamos – an unregarded small town in which a phenomenon is mapped which can change almost everything.

Elias himself knew that he was not researching something small. One of his most wide-ranging sociological ideas he called 'the civilising process'. What he and Scotson picked apart in Winston Parva was powerful enough to let him analyse and document the rise of 'civilisation' across continents and centuries. Something big enough to power the muggle-wizard economy for many generations.

If we take an elite which, to outsiders, has 'been there for generations' – for example board directors of major British companies – it is easy to transpose Elias and Scotson's account.

Newcomers arrive and encounter a barrier which feels just like a glass ceiling – something which no one creates, plans to sustain or even 'sees', but proves as durable as a stone fortification.

But I think we're inspecting something even more pervasive than that. Forget history: suppose today a group of renegades starts a new trend – a brand new idea about what counts as good. They may have no coordination – simply independent kindred spirits determined to think differently about something. At some point, some of the pioneers come to know of each other; they meet; they compare ideas. They may well disagree and remain independent agents, but we have the nucleus of a group which knows, and knows of, each other. Others seek to join. Soap-opera stories circulate about relationships, affiliations and splits. Of course they are only of interest to true followers, so knowledge of them works as a badge, identifying them as followers. Now we have all the ingredients for an unplanned wizardry.

Who am I?

IN THE LAST SECTION we took a ride on a short section of academic highway and saw the possibility of explaining something about elites with the help of research into a nondescript part of lower-middle and working-class England. But if you don't mind, it's time to raise the stakes.

The academic highway works for and is built by scholars. They labour on it as part of a quest. Their quest is for truth backed by evidence and reason. For the rest of us, a highway paved and checked by experts is convenient, but it puts 'us' in the comfort of an observation vehicle looking at objects through a scientific window. The objects are 'them' (elites, the muggle crust or the people who lived in Winston Parva). That's useful and safe, but now we need something more personal, like my encounter with mothers carrying babies on the streets of Mumbai (*see page 33*). They were not objects, and neither was I. Elites isn't just about different kinds of 'them': I want to show you that our subject is 'us' – whatever our social standing.

In other words, we're still searching for truth, but a truth which is more intimate than a diagram in a social sciences textbook. What is our quest about? Let's get some help from the searching which drives the Harry Potter stories.

One clue comes near the end of JK Rowling's seven-part series. Rowling herself says that she 'waited seventeen years' to write two lines in particular. After Harry sacrifices himself and awakens in the limbo King's Cross, in his last moments of conversation with Albus Dumbledore he asks:

> 'Tell me one last thing,' said Harry. 'Is this real? Or has this been happening inside my head?'
>
> Dumbledore beamed at him, and his voice sounded loud and strong in Harry's ears even though the bright mist was descending again, obscuring his figure.
>
> 'Of course it is happening inside your head, Harry, but why on earth should that mean that it is not real?'[15]

Rowling wrote more than 4,000 pages of story in order to have Harry ask Dumbledore, 'Is this real?' So it's beyond doubt that hunger for truth is part of the heartbeat of the story which she wanted to tell. Without being bitten by that quest myself, I would never have made it through many daunting volumes trying to follow the ideas of Elias and Bourdieu. (Bourdieu agrees with Dumbledore: 'Social reality exists, so

---

15   John Granger with Gregory Bassham in *The Ultimate Harry Potter and Philosophy*, ed. Bassham, pp. 185-6 (John Wiley 2010).

to speak, twice: in things and in minds, ...outside and inside of agents'[16].)

But if Harry's quest had been for intellectual truth alone, those 4,000 pages would have attracted a small fraction of their actual readership. Of course we lap up the adventure, colour and excitement, but we can find those in lots of places. What keeps us glued is Harry's quest to discover himself. Harry wants to discover who he is and can be, including what he means to others. Adolescence is a time for exploring identity – casting the familiar aside in order to find parts of ourselves whose existence is only rumoured. A quest like this can't be done from an armchair in your comfort zone. Harry had to get off his butt and put himself at risk.

Who says that adolescence should be the only time for this? By raising the stakes I mean imagining that right now might be another time in your life for casting the familiar and safe aside in order to find parts of yourself whose existence is (at least when we start off) only rumoured. In return, I hope to help you understand success. In the process, we will unpick the magic trick of elites, in a way which shows how the trick involves all of us.

So now we are off on a quest like Harry's. This is the rumour: what if the dominant Western understanding of what it is to be an individual isn't quite right? That would be something, wouldn't it? If we cracked that, fundamental change in the world would be inevitable. But this is nonsense, isn't it? We have learned too well that while our world may be social, we are its atoms. *I* choose. *I* decide. *I* think, therefore *I* am.

16   Pierre Bourdieu and Loïc Wacquant, *An Invitation to Reflexive Sociology*, Polity Press 1996, p. 127.

Whoa! A mistake in the blueprint for being an individual which I grew into? That's like imagining a 'mistake' in the five-times-table. Where did that idea come from? In answering this question, I can also illustrate the idea of parts of myself being buried in others who are different – specifically others in India, China and Africa.

India appears in this story through the Mumbai construction workers who propelled me out of a world I had come to know very well. They couldn't have been more different from me, but (with full credit to the committed preparation of Leaders' Quest) I had an encounter with the other which told me something unexpected about myself: that I could, and had to, jump off the salaried hamster wheel and explore the unknown. Strangers held one of the pieces of my identity. It was more important to me to be brave and to understand things than to be powerful.

I am too close to the Chinese half of my identity to be able to see it properly: if you want to know about it, you will need to ask others. They have those pieces of my jigsaw puzzle. In my growing up, being mixed-race swamped my understanding of myself, making what is specifically Chinese hard to pick out.

One example of how being mixed-race showed up for me came when I turned fifteen. I was sent to complete my school education at St Paul's, the public (in other words private) school in west London. I was a boarder: my family remained in Hong Kong, which at the time made low-cost shirts and plastic toys. These arrived in Britain labelled 'Empire Made'. At some point in my early weeks I transgressed some rule. The punishment decided on by the prefects (students with disciplinary responsibilities a year or two older than me) was to write a few hundred words on the theme 'Empire Made'. That was me, of course, with an English father employed by the Colonial Service and a Chinese mother.

From being mixed-race I know I have a natural curiosity about boundaries and the in-between spaces between groups. From the prefects and the culture of which they were a part (they were school wizards, really) I probably took the sting of feeling looked down on, of being a muggle. As I said previously, the word 'muggle' stings, like lemon juice on a cut.

My wife Trish and I first encountered Africa in the late 1980s through Nick Hayward. He is now a deputy director of safety and security in the South African province of Mpumalanga. At the time, Nick was a black activist in his early twenties, brought to Britain for his own safety and hosted by our church. He told us about his friend Raymond, who had been driven around for several hours by the South African police on rough roads before being taken to hospital for an operation. He died after hospital staff left scissors inside him.

Trish led our involvement in South Africa. In 2020 she received the Archbishop's Peace with Justice Award for her work. Along the way we encountered *ubuntu,* an African concept which I heard in translation as 'I exist because you exist'.

I didn't study *ubuntu*; it studied me. Years passed, crowded with common and less common experiences of life in London and, in time, buying a house in Johannesburg. Slowly *ubuntu* changed from an intriguing curiosity into a discomfort, a pea under the mattress of civilisation on which I slept. It took centre-stage in 2007 as I looked for doctoral programmes which might scratch my itch. Ralph Stacey and his colleagues at the University of Hertfordshire introduced me to Western thinkers (Bourdieu and Elias among them), who had explored with rigour the idea that individuals are not atoms, the collision of which makes up society. They pondered things the other way around: what if individuality emerges when we have a sufficiently complex society? As soon as I read the programme's prospectus I filed my application.

HUMAN BEINGS ARE INDEPENDENT, AUTONOMOUS AND SELF-CONTAINED

Grow up

To BE AN ADULT is to have one's shit together: to be an autonomous, self-contained being. My life might be straightforward or a puzzle, but if it is a puzzle, all my pieces are right here on my sofa, probably inside my head, definitely inside my bag of skin. All this is obvious.

By now this book has laid a lot of groundwork for shifts in the obvious. Specifically, we have explored a bunch of lessons which have the following property: they are not just true in an abstract way but vital to believe and act upon if you want to develop. Until you reach a point where there's a flip.

Up to now the development has been from muggle to wizard. Suppose now that the eleventh lesson is like the previous ten, but we have upped the stakes: the game is no longer muggles and wizards, but becoming fully human. Stick with me: from the beginning this book has been about 'up'. Now we're bringing in 'growing up'. (Remember that to see how a magic trick works, watch like a hawk long before the drum roll.)

Suppose autonomous individuality – something which we all have to nail and practise as children in order to 'grow up' – at a certain point flips to a bigger, opposite truth: the idea that human existence is not individuality but connection. In the eleventh lesson let's call the concept of individuality 'aloneness' and the flipped idea 'withness'.

Without the ten lessons in front of us, at this point we would be stuck. Aloneness and withness are opposites: it would be 'obvious' to us that only one can be right. No question about it, Western civilisation has plumped overwhelmingly for aloneness. The philosopher Descartes thinks that the only place from which to judge the existence of anything else is a solitary mind, a chamber of pure mental aloneness. ('I think, therefore I am.')

But the time we've spent on the ten lessons opens up the possibility of making a different claim: that without spending years buying into aloneness and learning what it teaches, we would fail to become individual humans (the eleventh lesson); but that without discovering withness (the flip) we will fail to become fully human individuals.

Let's look again at growing up. I have to pinch myself to remember the industrial quantities of aloneness which civilisation injects. From day one in school we live through the calling out or writing down of our names (the talismans of our existence) and getting report cards on what we have accomplished alone, academically or physically. Were you called to the front to speak alone, to be praised or punished alone? Not forgetting the special fear which goes with being called to go into the doctor's examining room alone.

Our civilisation-factories give pride of place to academic examinations, at school and university. These are special moments where the irony is entirely lost on us: fragile adults-in-the-making *herded together*, invigilated to make us *alone in a crowd*, our names checked, our futures solemnly dependent on making and keeping a vow of aloneness. *This is all my own work,* I declare, and in return I receive what seems to be a ticket to an adult self: a piece of paper to help me compete (alone, of course) in the working world.

The working world doubles down on the eleventh lesson (pay reviews, promotions or incantations of our name in dispatches), how easy it is to notice and congratulate ourselves on the solitariness of our achievements. But the propagation of aloneness by the civilisation-factory doesn't limit itself to the workplace. The eleventh lesson is built into how we are taught – especially in this age of technology – to produce and consume sport, music, entertainment and culture in all its forms. We adore the 'selfie'; we say 'look at me!'

Our civilisation is blazing trails in exploring emotionally, not just scientifically, how to be pregnant alone. But, you may be wondering, surely one proof of aloneness has been with us for all time – the aloneness of death.

Despite having a Christian faith, for most of my life I have taken as both obvious and piercing the reflection in Jackson Browne's song 'For A Dancer' that in the end there is one dance we do alone.

Only recently have I come to question whether this thought isn't the apogee of social programming. Whether or not anything comes 'after', death is the only human experience which we are guaranteed to share with every human who has ever lived. What a staggering party piece the invigilators in our minds pull off: to throw all of humanity together and, like their role models in examination halls, turn it into an experience of aloneness.

When I started as a writer, I thought of writing books, especially creative ones like novels, as projects of intense aloneness. This thought continued until Diana Nyad's 2013 TED talk 'Never, ever give up'[17] helped me notice differently. An endurance swimmer, at sixty-four she became the first person to complete the 100-mile open-water swim from Cuba to Florida. She recounts how she laughs when people ask her, 'And you do it alone?' She tells them how many people it involves, not least the crew who spend days and nights with her crawling over the ocean's face in a small boat which the rules do not allow her to touch, giving her drinking water. Now the reality of writing shows up for me quite differently. Right now, I'm spending between four and six hours a day alone working on a re-write of this book. I'm on my own, including many evenings, but am I writing this book alone? No, it's an intense team effort – just look at the 'Acknowledgements' page – although for many years I thought the answer was 'yes'. Was I wrong about dying too?

What might the idea that 'existence is connection' look like? For this idea to take off, we'd have to be able to join it up with important human experiences of not-existing because not-connected. Here the work we have done on elites comes into its own. Elites not only create the experience of not existing for those who are outside them, but now we can understand a key feature of their structure.

On page 149 Faiza Shaheen captured vividly the experience of not-existing because not-connected. It is a common experience reported by women in male-dominated meetings, often in the piquant form of proposing a solution which is taken up with acclaim some time later when proposed *as if for*

---

17   https://www.ted.com/talks/diana_nyad_never_ever_give_up

the first time by a man.

The other side of the coin now becomes obvious: wizard realms are stranger-free in order to function as realms of assured connection. Two wizards are always connected; to be a wizard is to always be known or known of, and to know or know of in return. If the sought-after status of being a wizard is any guide, then this might be 'peak human experience'. In their realms wizard identities suffer no blackouts or dropped signals, which is why the signature expression of wizard indignation is, 'Do you know who I am?!'

But to describe assured connection as assured existence is still a leap. Let's try. On page 147 I used a Scrabble set as an analogy to describe what happened at Winston Parva. I pictured the established and the newcomers as two handfuls of Scrabble tiles, the first closely connected by common knowledge and history, the second not connected to the first tiles or to each other. In other respects the tiles were identical. What Elias and Scotson observed was that even after years of being shaken together the tiles in the first handful retained their mutual connection in a way which tiles in the second handful found difficult to join. To describe this another way, the established at Winston Parva enjoyed assured connection (that's what makes an environment stranger-free). Newcomers threatened that.

Can Scrabble give us a clue as to what human life would be like if the eleventh lesson contained a flip, and aloneness was replaced by 'withness'? Imagine that we are all living Scrabble tiles. Each of us tries to discover the identity written on our faces, but the only way we can do this is by discovering our pattern of connection with other tiles. If you make intelligent connections with lots of other tiles (and the language of our universe is English), then you might reckon to be an 'E'; at the other end of the spectrum I might be a relative loner, such as 'Q'. The only way to find this out is through experience, interacting with as many different tiles as possible – in other words to venture out of your comfort zone, as Harry Potter does.

If I stick closely with a small group of tiles that I have known for some time (the trap for elites and the established in Winston Parva), I leave undiscovered a large part of who I am. This sentence is intellectually clumsy, but the point is too important for prissiness: what if parts of all of 'us' are scattered, waiting to be discovered in interactions with 'them'?

Notice that although an E connects with many more tiles than a Q, the central point is that *connection is existence* for both of them: there's no meaning to being a Q or an E except as part of the alphabet of a living language. You can't be a hermit without a group to be a hermit from.

So now we have some mind-teasing thoughts to play with. Do many of us try to get 'up there', where the wizards are, because we crave the experience of connectedness, of identity which never fails (an idea which finds an echo in the Christian concept of heaven)? Are elites our attempt to create that heaven on Earth? For the 'assured identity' of human elites is as fallible as any other human creation and comes with a big price tag.

What success turns out
to mean for me

'MY LIFE MIGHT BE straightforward or a puzzle, but if it is a puzzle, all my pieces are right here on my sofa, probably inside my head, definitely inside my bag of skin.'

Those words opened the last chapter, spelling out the perspective of the eleventh lesson (aloneness). According to a different perspective – withness – parts of me might be buried in other people. What does that feel like, concretely? Even if we carry all the pieces of ourselves around in our bags of skin, there's no guarantee that we can fit them together on our own. Carrying everything with you in your own bag may not be a sign of strength: it can signal being homeless.

The point of this chapter is to say something about what withness feels like, and to answer (as best I can) two further questions: what do I really want, and why do I want it? Writing this book has led to personal 'aha!'s which I hadn't been expecting; none bigger than the one prompted by writing this chapter. Suddenly the meaning of a memory which I had carried for forty years fell into place, and with it deeper insight into what kind of success I have been stumbling after all this time.

In this instance, the 'suddenly' happened over lunch one day in an exchange between myself, the theologian Sam Wells, who has written extensively about 'being with', and management professor David Sims, who coined the term 'withness'. But first, let's get a handle on this particular memory. To do this I'm going to jump out of my own bag of skin and watch alongside you, the reader, as we reconstruct what happens to my younger self.

A Marquis of Granby pub stands there today, camped then as now on a cramped triangular site a minute's walk from Trafalgar Square. On the Friday evening we find the person we're here to observe, the London newspaper *The Standard* costs 15 new pence and making a telephone call from the vicinity means using coins inside a red Tardis covered in business cards for 'models'.

The man is in his early twenties, six-foot-two, with curly dark hair. His pin-stripes, white shirt and briefcase could have come from Coutts, the private bank around the corner, but his fairly cheap glasses and *The Guardian* newspaper suggest a junior civil servant sinking a TGIF pint. He's on his own. Up close we see that the curls are permed (it is the 1980s). We take a chance on his mood to ask if he's waiting for anyone. He speaks. Words come out like upmarket supermarket vodka, fine for polite company, geographically colourless but thick with years of educational fermentation. He says he's fine, not waiting (even on a Friday night) for anyone or anything. He has no clue that what is about to happen will remain with him for years to come.

What happens is very sweet. The pub doors open to two lads his age from Liverpool. They're in sweatshirts, visiting London but not for football (otherwise they would have been with mates). They're at a loose end and fancy a bit of a pub crawl. For some reason they get talking to the suit at the far end of the bar, and the three of them go off together and have a great time. That's it: no asking to borrow money, no throwing up, no sex, no drugs, no stolen wallets or lost briefcases, no trouble – just quite a few pints and a brilliant night of 'withness'.

They swap names and the young man writes down which train they will be catching in the morning (civil servants write stuff down). But maybe the Liverpool lads oversleep, or maybe they didn't tell the young man the right train, because even on his trek to Euston station in the morning to say goodbye, he already guesses that they won't be there. If withness is difference transcended, it has only been for a while.

The exchanges were utterly ordinary, whereas stuck in the young man's memory for forty years is its specialness. 'No way could it have been ordinary!' he exclaims. 'Forty years on I can barely croak my way through a 'lads' conversation; back then I was so much worse!'

He badly wants us to understand something, we can hear that in his voice, but we're unconvinced. These days the man is so socially polished in professional settings that we might call him waxed. Why invent a made-up disability? But one by one his forefinger strikes potential conversation topics off an imaginary list.

'Sport – not interested. Don't know it, don't play it, can't talk it, can't fake it. That goes for pub sports too, like darts and billiards. Flirtatious glances, handing out scores on eye-candy – zero out of ten. Pop music – a bit, but nothing cool.

'I left Cambridge with gaps in my social skills as large as the egg-boiling hole in my father's culinary repertoire. My early adult world was thick with electric fences, obscure social limits which I couldn't get my hands on. Walls I couldn't see decided what kind of person would take what other kind of person seriously. That evening the Liverpool lads and I visited several pubs and talked effortlessly. For some reason – for a few hours – the walls weren't there, for them or for me.'

Although the feeling of that conversation never fades, forty years will pass before he can make any headway analysing his experience. Someone hands him David Sims' word 'withness'. Now he can say this about what made the evening unforgettable: 'It was a feeling of delight: the delight of discovering that someone wonderful exists, someone with very different clothes and accent and outlook on life. And this wonderful person can't think of a better thing to do than to be with you, and being with you makes them happy. I guess it's intimacy freed from need, manipulation or fantasy. Intense relationships are an obvious place to look for withness, but the togetherness you find there is often corrupted by those things. You can certainly find withness in friendship, but our civilisation doesn't treasure friendship.'

At the time the young man could not see it, but now

'withness' appears to have run through his life like a massive river. Now he sees years of therapy as a long hike, creating withness within: the amazed delight of discovering wonderfully different fragments inside himself, which slowly realised that they could find no better thing to do than to spend a lifetime with each other. He is talking about the amazed delight of discovering that someone wonderful exists. That 'someone' is himself.

Marriage and sustained friendship were more varied, erratic walks over the same hills. Most likely he chose not to have children because he craved relationships rich in withness, which the needs, manipulation and fantasies of parents or infants can squeeze out.

After working in government, he became a headhunter – a kind of recruiter. He spent eighteen years learning about wizard-making and boundary-crossing. A recruiter is thrown into very private conversations with individuals and organisations, but often to transactional ends. Latterly as a coach, withness became his stock in trade. Telling the story like this makes his changes of direction seem obvious; however, they were anything but.

Why the socially awkward teenager with a fierce mind studies mathematics (his father's and grandfather's subject at university) is unsurprising. But mathematics and fierce minds turn out to be socially electrified fences. They split the world into the chosen few (gifted but weird) and the mistaken many (their biggest mistake being so sure that complex ideas are beyond their grasp). He hates that division. So, at nineteen, he writes and publishes his first book, *Certificate Mathematics Explained*. Having few distracting options in terms of girlfriends, sports, music etc – see above – helps with this budding career.

During his twenties his passion to connect by communicating deepens. There are many years of therapy. Later a doctorate affects his writing in two ways: the research method involves practising ways of narrating which promote withness, and thanks to individuals like Bourdieu, new ways to understand social division explode in his head.

Discovering that you can understand algebra or balance sheets is like watching a high-quality science programme, or being in the jury box for a complex trial. Your mind opens, but the wizard-like explainer keeps the upper hand. Being offered new tools to explore social division in ordinary life is something else. Each of us has years of lived experience and fragments of insight, and none of us has anything more. We have more choices. We can construct alternative explanations. For example, we can conclude that the once-young man is an unfortunate idiot.

We might decide this because we see someone who grew up abnormally alone, abnormally sensitive to social barriers (some of which he will have fantasised) and abnormally driven to use his brain power to satisfy his cravings for our attention. Withness, existence as connection and the transcending of difference: important truths in his world may be idiocies in ours. We may be the fully adult, self-contained individuals who cracked autonomy in a way he did not.

Or we might find fragments of our own life buried in his. Then we might look at our shared world with new eyes. For example, we might look anew at the signature social interactions of our twenty-first-century culture. Our world may make new sense as a place where subliminally *we know that existence is connection, but we have forgotten the kind of connection* — withness — *we need*. Water, water everywhere, nor any drop to drink. Connection, connection is everywhere, but something is not quite right. The internet embodies the proposition that 'connection is existence' but suggests that we can have connection for free. Or take celebrity: a hollowed-out wizardry, the exclusivity of knowing and being known to others who are themselves known, but without merit.

The encounter in the Marquis of Granby lands in the young man's life like the obelisk in Kubrick's movie *2001*. It doesn't move or explain itself. Perhaps it means nothing; perhaps it means everything. Writing a book forty years later, he grasps an understanding.

The magic show
of elites

LET'S PUT THE MAGIC SHOW of elites together, reminding ourselves how it works from different seats in the theatre. The artisans and muggles are in the cheap seats. The muggle crust are in the front stalls. In the spotlight are the wizards. They know, or know of, each other.

The trick to be accomplished is the belief in all these groups that wizardry is the ultimate flowering of talent and hard work, when the truth is more complicated. Ladies and gentlemen, do we have any muggles in the audience tonight? A lot, excellent! Let me start with you: yes, young man, you in the gods. We've not met before, have we? We don't want anyone thinking that this is a set-up. So in your work, would you by and large agree that if you want to get on, you need to work hard and develop your skills? Excellent! And how about you, madam, in the dress circle: would you say the same?

Very good. We're all singing from the same hymn sheet.

But what about the muggle crust? If you would, sir, step out into the light where we can see you. Lovely. And is it hard work and some quite special abilities that have got you where you are today? And do you think about rising higher still?

Ladies and gentlemen, tonight we are in for a treat, because a wizard has volunteered to answer our questions. (Applause.) I wonder, ma'am, do you have any inspiring words of advice for someone who might be sitting in the theatre wondering whether one day the spotlight might be on them? (The wizard tells an affecting personal story.) Thank you so much for that moving story about learning to work hard and to believe that anything is possible.

The deepest magic lies in convincing the muggle crust of this, which is why we focused on them in Part Two. They are smart, and up close and personal with wizards daily. However, if only true believers in the ten lessons can make it into the muggle crust, that is half the battle.

The other half is getting wizards to keep the secret. Believing that their own hard work and brilliance got them to the top will come naturally. The tricky part is how to pass on the lesson flips, the change in the game and why this knowledge is for wizards only. This is where induction through apprenticeship (much of it subconscious) and the fact that wizardry is an extended community kicks in. There are no secret oaths or blueprints, any more than there were in Winston Parva. Learning who belongs and what it takes to belong are deeply ordinary, human processes.

For muggles, the first ten lessons of this book work like a magician's cane rapping on the sides of a wooden box:

nothing dodgy, fair principles which apply as far as the eye can see. Muggles believe in these principles.

The trick is a bit different for artisans. Their world seems more precarious than fair. Still, for those who want to climb, the ten lessons offer the best chance of getting on. Casting an eye around the more expensive seats, it seems that the muggle crust and the wizards believe the same. There is no sign of another game going on. In which case it follows that the whole show is a meritocracy, and the wizards are the best of the best.

Something else is worth noticing. Presented with a wizard, often the occupants of the cheap seats cheer particularly loudly and throw extra large bouquets of admiration at their feet. Why? Unlike the muggle crust, the occupants of the cheap seats feel pretty ordinary, not special at all. Yet they lavish such specialness as they have on those who already have a lot. The idea of withness offers a clue.

If withness is correct, a faint awareness may flicker inside us that important parts of ourselves may be buried in other people. The flicker rarely makes it into conscious thought, because years in the civilisation-factory have broken us on the opposite principle (aloneness: being independent and self-contained). But if important bits of me are buried in other people, then which other people? If I appear to be at the bottom of the heap, then surely not my family and workmates in the cheap seats, who, to be frank, look even more ordinary than me. Why not a wizard, you say? You mean the ones on the stage. That one... Maybe I can see some resemblance. Actually, she's a bit special, don't you think? Now you mention it, I can see the resemblance.

The name of this floor show is charisma. Charisma is the magic power which persuades most of us that we haven't got it. For different reasons it makes both the cheap seats and the muggle crust deliver gifts of specialness and admiration to wizards. The receiving end of these gifts feels like this: if I'm on stage, what's going on is that I was always pretty damn good, but now my brilliance has been recognised. The muggle crust call the giving end of the transfer imposter syndrome: I'm not good enough to be in the wings, next to the wizards, but no one's noticed yet. Cheap seats, front stalls, those on stage – all are convinced that wizards deserve to take a bow. Charisma is the misallocation of respect. Wizards deserve a good helping but we give them too much. The rest of us keep too little for ourselves.

I've mentioned being lucky enough sometimes to write by Lake Garda. One evening the sky above the Dolomites is clear, the moon high and the breeze occasional. Three kilometres across the lake yellow lights at the water's edge reveal the village of Limone. A thick ribbon of moonlight comes towards me across the water's inky surface. The ribbon is plainer than day. You could hold a ruler up to its straight edges. *The brilliance is there.*

That's the magic of meritocratic elites. It seems obvious where the brilliance is: we can point to it. The brilliance is a property of those individuals' specialness, just as the shimmering light appears to be a property of the water – and we can prove it. When the breeze disturbs the water, the brilliance disappears.

But that ribbon of light actually depends upon a much larger configuration involving the moon, the water and ourselves. Wherever I stand, the ribbon comes towards me.

Meritocratic elites have special talents, but charisma magnifies them to dazzling point. Elites are the top surface on the water, which plays a critical part in creating the spectacle of brilliance, but only as part of a larger configuration which involves us all. To make the analogy more exact, imagine that there is no sun, but that beside the lake the hills are covered in moonflowers: modestly luminescent flowers which track the moon in the sky, illuminate it and gaze wondering at the ribbon of brilliance which comes back towards them from the lake's surface. But this moon is lit by the flowers which track it.

So is this a picture with no magic in it? That depends on whether the moonflowers are magic. What do you think?

We ask ourselves, Who am I to be brilliant, gorgeous, talented, and fabulous? Actually, who are you not to be? You are a child of God. Your playing small does not serve the world. There is nothing enlightened about shrinking so that other people will not feel insecure around you. We are all meant to shine, as children do.

Marianne Wilson in *A Return to Love* (HarperCollins, 1992).

HOW TO CHANGE
ELITES
(Part Two)

THANK YOU FOR COMING with me on this journey.

Part Two of this book proposes that, left to their own devices, meritocracies produce wizards and muggles naturally. Wizards are not simply talented individuals, but belong to an elite, a village-like community in which all are known, or known of. 'Glass ceilings' is an apt phrase but misleadingly suggests something external which rising individuals bump into. Instead, Part Two describes socially-generated flips which are internal: a pattern of shifts in what's obvious inside the minds of aspirants and elites alike.

Part Three asks why this pattern exists. It suggests a deeply human and very ordinary answer – one which two sociologists spotted in a nondescript English town in the 1950s. I encountered their work thanks to a doctoral programme at the University of Hertfordshire which challenges the dominant idea, particularly pronounced in the Anglo-American West, that society is the complex interaction of atomic individuals. Encountering other cultures attracted me to this challenge.

Part Three goes on to suggest that the ideal of independent, autonomous and self-contained individuals (into which I grew up) might be a deceptive truth just like the ten lessons in Part Two. Not completely wrong, but true in a very particular way: true and essential for one stage of development, and then false – and a trap. Finally, Part Three shares how, in chasing down these answers, my understanding of my own life – particularly what I had been wanting from success – changed.

Fundamentally this book suggests that we misallocate

respect, giving too much to elites and not enough to the muggle crust and everyone else (including ourselves). If true, this point of view will have large consequences. I'm excited about that, because something is broken in our world. Some of the consequences will be unpredictable. But if changes flow from a debate which engages many minds, hearts and experiences (including yours and, for that matter, those of the women construction workers in Mumbai whom I met at the start of this journey), they will be better targeted and more potent than the ideas for changing our world which I describe now. But here's what I suggest.

Many people are already joining or creating _new movements and new types of organisations (including business) and communities_. Do it: and don't be disheartened if, as your new model gets traction, you bump up against a new wizard clique. This isn't a fail: it's part of being human. What might be a fail is doing nothing about the consequent glass ceilings.

As we discussed in Part Two, in _Humanocracy_[18] Gary Hamel and Michele Zanini suggest that we build organisations in which 'you [are] never given reason to feel inferior to the higher-ups' _(p. ix)_

I applaud the book's inspiring examples but I don't think this specific aspiration is possible or human. To exclude the possibility of any human being deserving, in the context of some shared activity, more respect than you is, in the end, to undermine the foundations of your own self-respect. This book has been about 'up': _to abolish 'up' is to try to live in a two-dimensional plane._

Surfing Soweto is an award-winning documentary made by

18   _Ibid._

South African film-maker Sara Blecher. She films the story of three teenage boys, Prince, Mzembe and Lefa, who live in the sprawling township of Soweto, where young black male unemployment is 75 per cent. The youngsters create and take up the activity of train surfing. They climb on, and under, the commuter trains which run to Johannesburg. They hang at impossible angles. They ride on top of the carriages facing backwards, ducking from memory to avoid being electrocuted or decapitated by overhead pylons. They become news and gain a following[19]. Sara builds a relationship with them. When she asks who is the best and gets the answer 'Prince', her respondents are not yielding to unnecessary hierarchy: they are showing us the 'up', the three-dimensional life, what is merit-worthy and more merit-worthy, in their activity: the meaning which they have created out of the near-nothing the rest of us have given them. Elites'R'Us, but we can adjust how we create and respond to them.

Whether an elite group is old or new, an obvious place for change is the point of entry – *wizard selection*. Selection decisions need to include outsiders as well as villagers, working together in an accountable process focused on the qualities being sought and how these can be demonstrated. But high-quality selection won't be enough. The muggle crust mindset encourages many of its members to think that they belong

---

19   As Bourdieu noted in the quotation on page 30, if you are not part of a particular society, if the structures of the game are not in your mind, the game will seem futile and ridiculous to you. But if your mind is structured according to the structures of the world in which you play, everything will seem obvious and the question of knowing if the game 'is worth the candle' will not even be asked.

(and will be happiest) where they are, that wizardry is not for them. And, for obvious reasons, wizards have a vested interest in new wizard talent being in short supply.

Once attracted and selected, future wizards will need experienced wizard-mentors. *Wizard-making needs to be done properly.* Those selected need their fair share of pixie dust (introductions to other wizards and help in establishing their profile) together with the other kinds of support – for example, experienced assistants or coaches – to help them break muggle habits and start creating magic. Their success is not for their benefit alone: far from it.

Move wizards on. Wizards who leave top jobs don't automatically stop being wizards, because wizardry is about personal connection and shared mindset. However, time limits on holding top roles keep things moving and create more opportunities for diversity. Above all, they counteract the poisonous effects of hubris and of senior wizards feeling that they know everyone who matters. Good governance already moves board members on from individual company boards, but to change the behaviour as well as the composition of the corporate elite we could limit every individual's total service on the largest boards: for example, a maximum of twenty years on FTSE 100 or equivalent boards (counting each board separately). Genuinely valuable insight would not go to waste; it would be on offer as advice and consultancy.

We need to *lead in ways which involve less make-believe and more mutual respect.* Exposing the elite game won't mean the end of society, but it could hasten the end of infantile society. We're adults, capable of being honest with each other about what our different varieties of leaders really do and why.

Mocking wizardry as merely a self-interested con game isn't fully adult; wherever we stand, it's a game in which we all participate. More of our heroic stories could be about the muggle crust. In full adulthood, the muggle crust could more confidently and robustly shoot down wizard nonsense, while working with wizards to do genuinely remarkable things.

Wizards gulled into effortless belief in their own superiority are also not fully adult. They could acknowledge that the magic they have is not magic at all, but something lent to them by all of us to do a job on our behalf. Wizards could admit the colour of their underwear.

Viewed with an organisational lens, many of these questions are human resource (HR) questions. That profession could play a decisive role in how things turn out. In the UK, the Chartered Institute of Personnel and Development has articulated an ambitious agenda which faces up to society's big questions. I hope this book plays a contributory role. *Board reviews* (which I do from time to time) are one of the few accountability checks on wizards within organisations, yet as part of the separation of wizards from muggles, HR directors are not automatically part of the client in the board review process. They should be (alongside the chair and the company secretary), and they should have stronger privileges to observe board discussions. The jobs wizards do are just jobs: elites are more ordinary than they would like us to think.

Back in the muggle crust, HR directors are ideally placed to challenge self-fulfilling, broad propositions about the *scarcity of talent*. Specific shortages can exist: however, a forced ranking performance-management system (the corporate equivalent of A levels by algorithm) is a self-fulfilling scarcity production system. In any organisation, it is the *HR director* who is most likely to be able to hold together the ordinary nature of the organisation's amazing people, and the amazing nature of their more ordinary colleagues.

But change needs to go well beyond workplaces: we need changes in *how we educate*. At its narrowest, everyone *growing up* has an ethical right to the best understanding we can give of how 'up' actually works – especially those aspects which expand or shrink what seems possible with our own lives, and dial up or dial down the respect which we give to others.

Education must stop functioning as the unstoppable power station of the aloneness-factory. It would look very different if it tried to *teach us that parts of ourselves are buried in diverse others.* Imagine university education being free for students who choose a higher-education milieu very different from the one they grew up in. Imagine degree courses being subsidised if they had new kinds of 'sandwich' years – for example years out in twinned, very different, kinds of educational establishments. Modern language degrees send students to live abroad, but in a sense every degree is a language degree. They simply construct in different ways the group whose language and way of looking at the world we decide to internalise.

Education has its heroes who have battled for years to keep the idea of education for life alive. It is part of a larger tragedy in British public services that control of our children's and their children's futures must now be wrested out of the hands of *a dangerous political wizardry* which, having beaten the life out of the public service muggle crust which serves it, now runs amok.

Large as these challenges are, you hold in your hands *two reasons to hope*. The first is that the muggle crust hides some of our best leaders, managers and professionals. Thanks to the way wizardry works, we mostly don't know who they are; but again thanks to the way wizardry works, many of them are clearer-eyed and less self-congratulatory than their wizard bosses. They are my hidden heroes. I hope this book increases their self-respect, power and career choices, and reduces their sense of being alone. Inside or outside their current jobs, if they choose to build a new world, they will be a remarkable force for making it happen.

The second reason is that the wizards' game depends on misdirection – on everyone in the theatre not spotting how, at the top level, the game changes, becoming something remarkably ordinary. If enough people discover what wizards do, the theatre will have to find a new production.

Many people influenced this book or read it in draft (*see page 205*). Some found that a friend noticed their concentration and, once they had got to the end, asked what the book was about. One of them said to me, 'I felt I had read the book and understood it, but struggled to answer crisply. Could you help?' I hope this helps:

The idea of human individuality which most Westerners grow up with may not be quite right. Human existence is connection. Thanks to not understanding this we give too much respect to elites and not enough to everyone else, including ourselves.

Rising and thriving without losing your soul

THIS HAS BEEN A BOOK about power. Power ripples through every part of it, from Henry's story in 'The room where it happens', through the dance between the muggle crust and wizards to the idea of capping individuals' service on major boards. However, we are commonly taught to think about power as a means by which individuals get more of what they want. Looked at like this, predicaments like that of Henry and Katharine become a bit like card games; getting smart about power means peering over their shoulders to see whether they could have played their cards differently. I referred to this previously.

This kind of thinking about power is dangerous. It mirrors – and so traps us in – the idea that individuals are self-contained atoms and society is the mess produced by their actions. We focused instead on how reality shows up for different players, particularly focusing on what they find obvious.

This allowed us to grasp the complex power play in Winston Parva. Speaking in the ordinary way about power, we might say that knowing each other and having a common history gave the town's established residents power over the newcomers, who had none of these things. But neither group planned, or particularly wanted, to 'do down' the others. The cards of power which the established residents held (largely unawares) played them, as much as they played the cards.

In order to skirt this 'aloneness' trap, we approached power by a less common route. In so doing, we've exposed and named the underlying problem. We can also point out some ways in which common approaches to power let us down in a dangerous way.

The first way to misread power, already discussed, is to stick with the assumption of aloneness: that individuals are self-contained autonomous agents. The second way is to leave unexamined what we individually want.

A bestseller on power is *The 48 Laws of Power* by Robert Greene[20]. The back cover says:

> Amoral, cunning, ruthless, and instructive, this piercing work distils three thousand years of the history of power into forty-eight well-explicated laws... this bold volume outlines the laws of power in their unvarnished essence...

Over 430 pages Greene advances propositions such as 'make all your accomplishments seem effortless' (law 30) and 'strike

---

20   Profile Books (1998).

the shepherd and the sheep will scatter' (law 42). The laws are illustrated with incidents from periods of history as diverse as early sixth century China BC, classical Greece or Rome, or Napoleonic times. Power is treated as how you can get more of what you want. Each law is offered as an objective insight into the human world which allows you to do that. What you want, what you use the laws to achieve, is your lookout; Greene sees no need to explore this.

But leaving whatever you want unexamined is a big fail. Some kinds of power are loud: to work they must be noticed (for example, threatening someone with a gun). Others are quiet, working best unnoticed (for example, nudging someone else to want what you want them to want). The internet is the largest nudging machine we have ever built. In this period of history, could anything be more naïve than assuming no one has tampered with what *you* want? Political competence has to include asking searching questions about what you want, and why you want it. That is the reason why *Elites* couldn't simply be 🔺 but had to include putting what I really wanted under the microscope.

Many books on power leave what you want unexamined. For example, Jeffrey Pfeffer, a wizard professor at Stanford Business School has written *Power: Why Some People Have It – And Others Don't*[21]. Like Greene he concentrates on the *how* questions:

> Your task is to know how to prevail in the political battles you will face. My job in this book is to tell you how. (p.5)

---

21   Harper Business (2010).

But towards the end of the book it becomes apparent that he does care what his readers want. Writing for (in my language) aspirant muggles and the muggle crust, Pfeffer doesn't want to see them bullied, overworked, made ill or otherwise taken advantage of as corporate saps. (Neither do I.) But he doesn't suggest, or show by example, that wants need to be critiqued before being acted on.

Thinking how autonomous individuals can get more of what they want without asking why they want it swallows whole a dangerous and very 'alone' idea of power.

It also rots our soul. Philosophers like Charles Taylor[22] argue that while animals have wants, we humans have more than this: we have *wants about our wants*. A dog may want meat, and we may want chocolate, designer jeans or freedom, but we judge our wants. Our wants may please us or displease us. Debates about these things are ethical debates. To be human may not involve having any particular set of ethics, but it certainly involves having ethical debates.

The danger to our souls doubles if our reading of power encourages us to treat people as things rather than persons. Scientific accounts do this twice, by presenting the person who speaks to us as an impersonal observer, and by presenting what is observed (people whom we try to manipulate) as a set of measured objects. Pseudo-scientific accounts offer the worst of all worlds, providing full-on depersonalisation without genuine scientific insight.

Greene rings all those alarm bells. More than 400 pages do not give him enough room to tell us anything of himself, or of any occasion when he attempted to apply one of his

---

22   See 'Appendix'.

own laws, or how he discovered them. The alternative approach which a guide to power can take is for the person to stand before us as a life-size, imperfect human; to tell us enough about themselves and what they have done, including mistakes, to let us make our own judgements; and to work hard at making their ethical foundations and motives plainly visible. *Elites* would have been dangerous without ▰ .

Understandings of power which will nourish your humanity and protect your soul: will not assume a world of autonomous, self-contained individuals; will teach that 'what I want' needs to be the beginning, not the end, of an exploration; and will work as hard as possible to be honest, authentic and vulnerable. A good example is Brené Brown's TED talk 'The Power of Vulnerability'[23] – at the time of writing viewed nearly fifty million times. Understandings like this can help all of us rise and thrive. *Elites* offers this kind of understanding.

When, instead, we grapple with power pseudo-scientifically, we inhale something much more dangerous to our souls than Niccolò Machiavelli's *The Prince*[24]. Why? In essence, that classic is A Mediaeval Prince's Survival Guide. Maurizio Viroli, professor of politics at Princeton University, writes in the introduction to the edition cited:

Contrary to the black legend of an atheistic or anti-religious Machiavelli, there is nothing in *The Prince* that goes against God or against what Machiavelli believed

23   https://www.ted.com/talks/brene_brown_the_power_of_vulnerability?language=en
24   Oxford University Press (2005); first published 1532.

to be true Christian moral and political teaching. *(p. xxxix)*

Today's atomised way of thinking of individuals would probably be incomprehensible to Machiavelli: *The Prince* was published a century before Descartes' 'I think, therefore I am'. *The Prince* has many 'how to' chapters (for example, 'How a prince should act to acquire esteem' *(XXI)*) but the author is open about having a moral goal, which is to promote a form of adult and republican Christianity. He even shows vulnerability, making his own position (at the time of writing an outcast from power) vividly clear.

END NOTES

REVIEWING
THE CLIMB

(Back at base camp)

Our journey revisited

Part Two of this book describes how meritocracies produce glass ceilings. Ten times we hike from the muggle valley to the top of a meritocratic mountain, noticing along the way how what is obvious changes. Part Two says that at the top of every such mountain we will find an often-invisible village: an elite whose members (wizards) find themselves with a shared and distinctive mindset and in a web of reciprocal connection.

Just like a real village, members of an elite, although connected, do not necessarily like or agree with each other. The web of connection is based on personal knowledge, knowing each other, knowing of each other, and knowing at one remove (perhaps I have not heard of you but with one phone call I can speak to someone who does). There is also knowledge in common, bound up with incidents in the soap opera of village life ('were you there when…?'). Importantly, this village only admits new members by consensus.

The nature of elites is rarely discussed out loud, even by their own members. The operations carried out in Part Two – for example, making sure that the opportunity to join is *not* open to all – mostly take place outside the realm of conscious notice. Unnoticed shifts in the obvious do most of the heavy lifting. The magic trick of elites is to convince many wizards and most of the rest of us that the game being played is merit all the way to the top. One of the trick's consequences is a misallocation of respect: wizards deserve some, but we (artisans, muggles and muggle crust) impoverish ourselves and give them too much.

Because many people work in organisations or activities which are – or try to be – meritocracies, what Part Two says can be tested. If you are in the muggle crust, you are the jury: do the flips in the first ten lessons help you make sense of your experience? We then looked at three action takeaways. How might you be more effective and more content with your achievements in the muggle crust? How might you become a wizard? Or change the system? Before making these choices, some self-inquiry may be helpful. We have seen many tricks played with the obvious: even if what you want looks obvious, perhaps it isn't.

If the mountain map in Part Two is true, Part Three asks 'why?'. In fact, this is just one of a Pandora's Box of big questions. Part Three suggests an answer which has nothing to do with elites being special: on the contrary, the research in Winston Parva describes something profoundly ordinary.

In Part Three I chase down this explanation as far as I can. I also try to show what not taking 'what I want' for granted might look like. The results include unexpected insights into my own hankering after 'success'. It turns out we are onto the trail of a very big question indeed: what does it mean to exist as a human being, to have one's own life? Will what seems 'obvious' let us down again?

I find that from an early age I have been sleeping with the ghost of Descartes. For most of my life I have understood that to be a person is to be an atom, of course interacting furiously with other atoms and at times deeply dependent on some of them, but when push comes to shove a grown-up individual, a soul, a uniqueness which is sovereign, independent, separate, alone. If I am the only one who has thought that way then the laugh is on me.

Another possibility is that we are tiptoeing towards a *civilisational mistake*. 'Civilisational' because it is so deeply rooted in Western (particularly Anglo-American) thought structures, intensified through education, and pandemic in its effects on human lives and happiness. 'Mistake' in such a specific sense that I do not believe an English word exists for it: a mistake in the specific sense of the ten lessons in Part Two. By no means through-and-through wrong, each one is a precept which has to be fully absorbed and believed in order to progress to the next stage. Until that stage the precept is a truthful guide, an essential compass. But then the lesson flips. Maybe *decept* could be a name for this kind of truth-proposition: deception and essential precept fused together.

If we revisit the glossary with which this book opened (*see page 13*), *decept* is not the only word which might usefully be added.

The idea that one individual cannot be said to exist without others is what I understand by *ubuntu*. Instead, parts of each of us are buried in other, especially different, people. I discuss this on page 155 and in the chapter which follows.

If we are not atoms but our existence relies on deep mutual connections with others, we can *experience non-existence* (which would otherwise be a paradox). Faiza Shaheen discovered this after appearing on *The Andrew Marr Show*, page 149. Accidentally or intentionally, but inevitably painfully, the social signal drops. I describe craving *assured identity*, where the dropped signal can't happen. This is the promise of some religions (notably Christianity) while refuted as a chimera or trap by others (notably Buddhism). Membership of an elite might be our closest manufactured substitute.

The most potent word in the glossary (it hides there undefined) turns out to be *respect*. Full human existence requires not just being rooted in a web of relationship but the dimension of 'up' in our lives: a sense that some things, ideas, actions or experiences are better than others; a making real – even if they cannot be made 'objective' or put beyond argument – of merit, quality and standards in our doings. Without 'up', *respect* is impossible: to respect something is to consider that it has some 'upness', that it is worth our time and attention. In a flat world with no 'up' – an animal-like world, replete with desires and threats but no accountability to standards – nothing is worthy and so we are not worthy. The source of *self-respect*, a crucial ingredient of fully human existence, is taking part in activities through which we together generate a sense of 'up'. The human magic is to be able to create this out of near-nothing, as with the train surfers in Soweto on page 182 or the women construction workers in Mumbai on page 33, who without knowing it, dispatched me on this quest.

And so, back to where we started, to the first word in the glossary. *Meritocracies* then turn out to be those meaning-making activities in which we focus in a particularly disciplined way on the kind of 'up' which we are creating together. Part of meritocratic discipline is openness and transparency. But openness and transparency are themselves forms of 'upness' which we make through what we do together, and so they come replete with blind spots, self-deceptions and manipulations. Don't phone up the manufacturers (ourselves) in dismay; take a bow for playing your part in a remarkable species-wide achievement. We have more power, and more choice, than we think. The magic available to all of us is the magic of being connected, of being human.

Suggested books

Two titles, both slim and highly readable, stand out for their relevance to the theme of elites. Michael Young's prophetic *The Rise of the Meritocracy* (second edition, 1994, republished in 2017 by Routledge) was originally published in 1958. Its form is a fictional analysis of English society set in 2034.

The Established and The Outsiders: A Sociological Enquiry into Community Problems by Norbert Elias and John L Scotson (whose second edition was also published in 1994, by Sage Publications) was originally published in 1965. The extensive introduction by Elias gives a clear sense of the larger sweep of sociological thought into which this study in Winston Parva fits.

Charles Taylor has provided a magisterial analysis of what it is to be a human self in *Sources of the Self: The Making of Modern Identity* (Cambridge University Press, 1989).

For the key ideas which surface as 'withness' (a term coined by David Sims), an excellent starting place would be Sam Wells' *A Nazareth Manifesto: Being With God* (Wiley Blackwell, 2015). A strikingly lucid writer, his focus here is what the lasting significance for us might be of the majority of Jesus' life (in other words, all the stuff which doesn't make it into the Christian creeds).

Lynsey Hanley has provided an excellent illumination of the artisan–muggle boundary and its associated power issues: *Respectable: The Experience of Class* (Allen Lane, 2016).

In analysing glass ceilings in the way I have, I don't seek to subtract anything from the specific obstacles experienced by women, people of colour or LGBTQ+ individuals. An example of powerful writing from these perspectives is the poetry and prose of Audre Lorde, for example, *Sister Outsider: Essays and Speeches* (Berkeley, 1984).

Although not used explicitly in this book, the concept of recognition as developed by Axel Honneth in *Struggle for Recognition: The Moral Grammar of Social Conflicts* (Polity Press, 1995; first published in German in 1992); *The I in We: Studies in the Theory of Recognition* (Polity Press, 2014); and others of his writings is fundamental to the way I have pitched both elites and withness.

The Honneth books are theoretical works in what one might describe as the marshland between philosophy and sociology, terrain also inhabited by Pierre Bourdieu. To pick one Bourdieu title is invidious but *The Logic of Practice* (Polity Press, 1990; first published in French in 1980) was influential for me.

Bourdieu's work can't be described as immediately

accessible. My colleague Rob Warwick and I provide our best shot at a 'near-plain English' account of Bourdieu's logic of practice (including *habitus*) as part of our book, *The Social Development of Leadership and Knowledge: A Reflexive Inquiry into Research and Practice* (Palgrave Macmillan, 2013).

MBA (Lightning Books, 2015), my first novel, is a partial exploration through satire and farce of what I describe in this book as the muggle-wizard boundary. The novel asks why so much of the world is managed by arseholes. My second novel, *Time of Lies* (Lightning Books, 2017), explores both the muggle-wizard and artisan-muggle boundaries.

Acknowledgements

Many people generously read and commented on this book or sections of it at different stages of its genesis – without of course acquiring responsibility for its content. With deep apologies for any omissions, these include: Cassandra Coburn, Paul Dyer, Clare Ella, Lynne Embleton, Jo Hill, Fiona Hiscocks, Gareth Jones, Jessica Kenny, Jane Kirton, Mark Lewis, Thabo Makgoba, Ian McIntosh, Kopano Mholo, Alice Newkirk, David Newkirk, Matthew Noyes, Alex Richmond, Chris Rodgers, Stefan Stern, Niall Trafford, Victoria Ward, Nick Wilkie, Hugh Willmott and Dillon Woods. Daniel ShenSmith provided legal advice and illuminated the history of the word 'muggle'.

It's been a privilege to journey as a writer with DARK, the writing group whose other members are Alison Donaldson, Rob Warwick and Kathy Jones.

My primary inspiration has been the hidden heroes in the muggle crust whom I have had the privilege to meet, coach or work with. Jo Hill has played a central and generous part in creating this book and, alongside Jonathan Morgan, provided invaluable comments and ideas on successive drafts. They have been muggle crust but I think are now wizards in their fields (I'll need to check their CVs to be sure).

A wizard within publishing, Dan Hiscocks put his soul into birthing and shaping the book. As publisher, editor and friend he has profoundly influenced the manuscript's two-year journey to its present shape. Dan founded Eye Books in 1996 because he believed in ordinary people doing extraordinary things. I was thrilled that both Martha Ellen Zenfell and Ruth Killick agreed to work with me again, Martha on editing and Ruth on publicity. Clio Mitchell's skill and commitment in completing the editing task were astonishing.

I hope that this book wears on its sleeve what it owes not just to giant thinkers such as Pierre Bourdieu and Norbert Elias, but the University of Hertfordshire Complexity and Management Centre – not least my late supervisor, Doug Griffin. I thank David Sims, Laura Empson and Hugh Willmott of the business school formerly known as Cass for generous intellectual inspiration and companionship.

Some of the foundations of this book are theological. The clarity with which Sam Wells has expanded 'withness' made a decisive contribution. The late David Beetge, Bishop of the Highveld, remains to me an outstanding example of a good wizard, as well as a friend and an introducer to *ubuntu*.

Since this book is about how we misallocate respect, let me heartily thank and pay respect to the women in Mumbai and the two lads from Liverpool – the tip of an iceberg of contributions to my life by individuals whose names I do not know.

Trish could have stopped believing in my 'magic' a long time ago but hasn't; thank you.